1000 FACTS ON
HORSES

ISBN-13: 978-0-7607-6084-0
ISBN-10: 0-7607-6084-5

Printed and bound in China

5 7 9 11 13 12 10 8 6 4

First Published in 2004 by Miles Kelly Publishing Ltd.,
Bardfield Centre, Great Bardfield, Essex, U.K., CM7 4SL

Editorial Director: Belinda Gallagher

Project Manager: Lisa Clayden

Designer: Neil Sargent, DPI Colour

Picture Research: Liberty Newton

Production: Estela Boulton

Americanization: Cindy Leaney

1000 FACTS ON
HORSES

Marion Curry

BARNES & NOBLE

NEW YORK

Contents

Key

 Development and anatomy

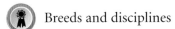 Breeds and disciplines

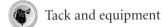 Tack and equipment

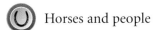 Horses and people

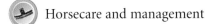 Horsecare and management

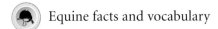 Equine facts and vocabulary

Contents

Contents

Development of the modern horse

- **Fossil evidence shows** that the horse's earliest ancestor can be traced back about 55 million years to *Eohippus* or the "Dawn Horse"—a small mammal about the size of a fox. It had four toes on its front feet and three on its hind feet.

- **Over millions of years**, this animal gradually developed three hoofed toes, and later a single hoof on each foot. It also evolved longer limbs that enabled it to move over a wide area in search of food and to escape predators.

- **These animals** were nomadic, roaming in herds for safety. As the horses traveled across the continents, the differing climates and terrain produced different kinds of horse.

- **The hotter climates** produced finer horses that could cope with the extreme temperatures, while those living in cold, mountainous areas were more ponylike.

▼ *The gradual evolution of the horse shows how it has adapted to changing conditions over millions of years.*

Eohippus

Mesohippus

Parahippus

- **Warm bloods** from hotter climates were noted for their speed, while the cold bloods from cooler climates were strong, calm, and hairy.

- **Mongolian tribes** were first to domesticate the horse about 5,000 years ago. The animals were kept for their meat and milk, and also used for transportation.

- **All domestic horses** in the world today are descended from these ancestors and are called *Equus caballus*.

- **For centuries**, horses have served man in agriculture and industry, as pack animals and transportation, and in warfare, leisure, and sports.

- **Today**, there are over 150 distinct breeds of horse and pony.

- **Horses who do not belong** to a specific breed can be categorized into types, such as hunter or cob. A hunter is any animal willing to jump freely and able to carry a rider for a full day on the hunting field, while a cob is often said to combine the best characteristics of a horse and pony, being strong, sensible, and calm.

Longer neck for grazing

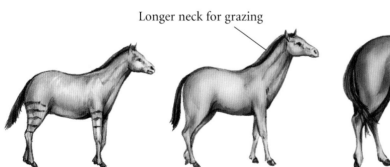

Longer legs for running

Merychippus　　　　*Pliohippus*　　　　*Equus*

Relatives of the horse

◄ *Donkeys can live for as long as 30 or 40 years.*

- **Horses belong** to the *Equus* family. *Equus* comes from the ancient Greek word meaning "quickness." Horses are mammals in the same family as zebras, mules, and donkeys. They all have a single toe or hoof.

- **The zebra family** is found in southern Africa—only three species survive. Each lives in different habitats and has differing patterns of stripes.

- **Zebras are highly gregarious animals**, congregating in large groups.

- **Female donkeys** carry their foals for 12 months before they are born—two months longer than a female horse.

- **The Quagga,** a variety of zebra, became extinct in the 19th century.

- **"Jack" is the name** given to the male donkey, "jennet" to the female.

- **Donkeys were first** domesticated about 6,000 years ago and are still used as work animals. They have developed strength and stamina, carrying heavy loads over long distances on little food or water.

- **The feet of donkeys**, like horses, grow continuously and need to be trimmed about every six weeks.

- **A mule** is a hybrid of a horse and a male donkey. A hinny is a cross between a female donkey and a horse.

- **Mules are noted** for their strength and good temperament.

▼ *Every zebra has a different pattern of stripes. It is not known for certain why they have this pattern. It may be to confuse predators, to help individuals recognize one another, or to keep their bodies at a comfortable temperature.*

Horse sense

- **Horses have** more highly developed senses of sight, hearing, and scent than humans.

- **Horses' eyes** are set far apart on either side of their head, which makes it possible for them to see in almost every direction at once—except directly in front of their nose and directly behind their tail.

- **Touch is one of** the most developed senses in horses. They can sense a fly landing on any part of their body and use their tail to flick it off. Horses respond to touch all over the body—especially on their ears and eyes.

- **Horses have large ears** that can move around and point toward sounds. Each one can rotate through 180 degrees.

▲ *This horse appears relaxed. Its ears show no sign of tension.*

- **A horse's ears can indicate** how it is feeling. Beware if they are laid back flat as this can show that the animal is feeling aggressive.

- **Horses are able** to recognize friends, both human and animal, by smell alone. Horses are also sensitive to smells in their environment, such as dung, dirty troughs, musty feed, bad water, and certain plants.

◀ *Most horses have dark colored eyes. This horse has a blue "walleye." A horse who is affected will probably have one walleye and one normal eye.*

- **The whiskers that grow** from a horse's muzzle and around its eyes are like an insect's antennae. They are used to feel nearby objects and should never be removed.

- **When a horse is cold**, it will feel cold to the touch behind its ears.

- **Horses have** a very good long-term memory. A horse will often remember where it got a fright and will continually shy at that place.

▼ *Most horses have four natural gaits: walk, trot, canter, and gallop. This mare and foal are showing a free-moving canter.*

...FASCINATING FACT...
Horses are attracted by sweetness and sugar.
Like humans, they will often reject sour, bitter,
and unusual tastes.

13

Conformation

- **Different breeds** of horses are defined by their conformation—their size or the shape of their body. Whatever the breed or type of horse, the whole outline should be symmetrical and balanced.

- **A horse's head** should be in proportion to its body—neither too big nor too small. A head that is too large unbalances the animal.

- **The feet** should be neat and the front and back pairs should be symmetrical.

- **Eyes should be large** and clear. They should not show large patches of white that could indicate the animal is frightened.

- **The back and hindquarters** should be strong and well muscled. The back should not be too long for the horse's height as this could result in weakness.

- **A parrot mouth** is where a horse has an overbite, the top teeth overhang the bottom teeth.

- **Cow hocks** are those which turn inward, while the back feet turn out. Bow-legs mean the feet turn inward.

- **A sway or hollow back**, where the horse's back dips markedly from the withers showing a prominent backbone, could be the result of old age or weakness.

- **A ewe neck** makes a horse look as though its neck is on upside down, with the strong muscles underneath instead of on top. This can make horses difficult to control.

● **Flat feet** may be the result of low heels. A horse with this condition can find it painful walking over rough ground, which in turn can lead to bruising and lameness.

▲ *In showing classes, judges look for well-proportioned animals who are excellent examples of their breed and fit for their purpose.*

Vital parts

- **Horses have an area** of about 14 ft (4 m) around themselves which they regard as their personal space. Only friends, horse or human, are allowed to approach more closely.

- **An adult horse's brain** weighs about 22 oz (650 g)—about half the weight of an adult human brain.

- **A horse usually has** 54 vertebrae in its backbone. Arab horses are the exception, having a slightly smaller number.

- **When galloping**, a horse supports all its weight on one hoof. It takes nine months to a year to grow a completely new hoof.

- **An adult horse** usually defecates approximately 5 to 12 times a day. Native ponies, both male and female, usually choose to keep their droppings in distinct areas and so maintain the maximum amount of pasture for grazing.

- **A horse's skeleton** is divided into two main sections: the axial skeleton—the skull, spine, ribcage, and pelvis, and the appendicular skeleton— the bones of the limbs.

▶ *A galloping racehorse can reach speeds of up to 45 mph (70 km/h).*

- **At rest, a horse** breathes between 10 and 15 times a minute.

- **Blood makes up** about 8 to 10 percent of a horse's total body weight.

- **At rest**, a horse's pulse measures 46 to 42 beats per minute. If frightened this can rise quickly to over 250.

- **Horses have 16 muscles** in each ear, enabling them to detect sound coming from any direction.

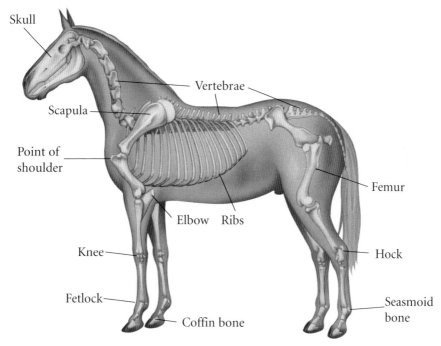

Skull

Vertebrae

Scapula

Point of shoulder

Femur

Elbow   Ribs

Knee

Hock

Fetlock

Seasmoid bone

Coffin bone

▲ *A skeleton of the horse, identifying the basic bone structures. The skeleton allows the horse to support its weight and protects its internal organs.*

17

Feet

- **Horses are odd-toed** animals, having only one toe or hoof on each leg.

- **In the wild**, horses wear their feet down naturally. Domestic horses, however, usually need to have their feet trimmed about every six weeks.

- **Horses that work** or travel on hard roads need their hooves protected by metal shoes. These need to be replaced every 4 to 6 weeks.

- **The person who** cares for a horse's feet is called a farrier.

- **To measure a horse** or pony's foot for shoes, take the measurement across the widest part of the foot and also from the toe to the heel. Front and hind feet may be different sizes.

- **Hooves are made** of keratin, a protein that is the same substance as hair or human nails.

- **The frog** is the rubbery wedge-shaped part on the underside of a horse's hoof. It helps absorb shock as its hoof hits the ground, and prevents slipping.

- **Mud can absorb** moisture from the hoof wall and make it brittle.

- **A horse often paws** the ground with a front foot prior to rolling. Pawing can also be a sign of frustration.

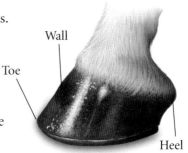

Wall

Toe

Heel

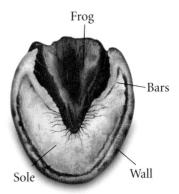

Frog

Bars

Sole

Wall

▲ *The outside layer of the hoof is insensitive and allows for shoes to be nailed on.*

...FASCINATING FACT...
Horseshoes are considered lucky and replicas are
often carried by brides on their wedding day.

Traditional front horseshoe

Traditional hind horseshoe

Remedial shoes to help alleviate foot problems

Lightweight racing plate

▲ *Different styles of horseshoe can be fitted. The shape and materials are chosen to suit the needs of the horse.*

Height

- **The height of horses** is measured in hands. One hand is equal to 4 in (10 cm). If a horse measures 15.2 hh (hands high), then it is 67 in (157 cm) high.

- **The measurement** of a hand was originally based on the width of a man's palm and was later standardized as 4 in.

- **The measurement** is taken from the ground up to the withers, the highest point on a horse's shoulder.

- **For an official measurement**, the horse has to have its shoes removed. The horse is on flat, level ground and a vet uses a measuring stick to gain an accurate measurement.

- **An important height is 14.2 hh**. Below this height animals are classed as ponies, while those over this height are horses. However, sometimes this rule does not apply.

- **An Arab is always called** a horse even if it is only 14 hh, and polo ponies are always called ponies even if they are 15 hh.

◀ *Small breeds of pony are often measured in inches or centimetres.*

...FASCINATING FACT...
The tallest horse was a Shire called Sampson.
He measured just over 21.2 hh.

- **Falabellas** are the smallest breed in the world, measuring around 30 in (76 cm). They are said to be good-tempered and friendly.

- **Some competitions** such as junior showjumping or showing classes are organized by height.

- **Height is not the only difference** between horses and ponies. Ponies usually have different conformation and may have a bouncier stride.

▶ *Heavyweight draft horses, such as Shires and Clydesdales, are among the tallest breeds of horses, often reaching in excess of 18 hh.*

Markings

- **Markings** are areas of white on a horse's body and some have particular names, such as a star or blaze. Markings are used to identify animals.

- **Horses have feathers**—clumps of hair growing at the back of their fetlocks. Some breeds have very fine, short hair while others, such as Shire horses, are famed for their long, thick feathers.

- **Horses have chestnuts**—horny plaques that grow on the inside of each of their legs.

- **White socks** that extend above the knee are called stockings. A snip is a small area of white above the top lip or around the mouth.

- **A prophet's mark** or thumb print is a small dimple or indent on the horse's skin, usually found around the neck or shoulder. It is said to be lucky.

- **Some white hair** growths are not natural markings. They are the result of old injuries, perhaps due to an accident or pressure marks caused by an ill-fitting saddle.

▼ *White leg markings are described by using the points of anatomy that the white hair covers.*

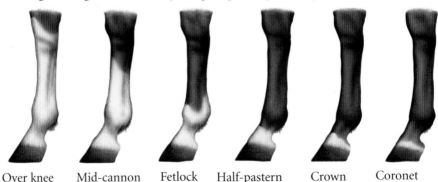

Over knee   Mid-cannon   Fetlock   Half-pastern   Crown   Coronet

Star

Stripe

White face

- **Ermine marks** are dark spots on top of markings just above a hoof.

- **Pink-skinned horses** can suffer from sunburn, particularly on areas where their hair is fine or thin, such as the muzzle. Sun-protection creams should be used to prevent damage.

- **Horses can be security-marked** on their skin, usually by freeze-marking under the saddle area or on the neck under the mane.

Blaze

Snip

▲ *Different patterns of face markings are used to help identify individual horses.*

> ...FASCINATING FACT...
> Some horse breeds still show primitive leg stripes and dorsal stripes along their backs.

Coats and colors

- **Horses can be** either the same color all over (whole colors) or a mixture of colors (broken colors).
- **The most commonly recognized** whole colors are bay, black, brown, chestnut, dun, cream, palomino, and gray. The broken colors include piebald, skewbald, roan, and spotted horses.
- **A palomino** is a light gold color with a light mane and tail.
- **Piebald and skewbald** are horses whose coats are made up of patches of either black and white, or white and another color, usually brown.

▼ *A well-matched team of six chestnut-colored horses, showing variation in mane color and face markings.*

- **Strawberry roan** and blue roan describe a mix of chestnut and gray, and black and gray hairs.

- **Light or dark bay** is brown with a dark mane and tail. The amount of dark or light hair in the coat determines which type of bay.

- **Chestnut horses** vary from reddish brown through to deep reddish gold. They are often said to be quick-tempered although there are no proven links between a horse's color and its temperament.

- **Spotted horses** have gray coats spotted with black or brown.

- **All white** horses are called grays.

- **Horses that work** during the winter are often clipped to remove their thick winter coats. This allows them to keep cool while working. Clipped horses need to be rugged to provide protection against the elements.

▲ *Dun-colored horses usually have dark manes, tails, and legs. The coat is a sandy color, with different shades classed as yellow, blue, or mouse.*

Stallions and geldings

- **A stallion** is a male horse capable of siring foals.

- **A gelding** is a castrated or gelded male.

- **Male horses** reach maturity from about two years onward, but are known as colts until they are four years old.

- **In the wild**, two year-old colts are driven off by the stallion to form their own bachelor groups. They will stay together before attempting to steal mares of their own.

- **The stallion in charge** of a group of mares will round them up and fight off any advances by rival stallions.

- **In domestic situations**, a stallion is usually kept away from both mares and geldings.

- **Stallions require** special handling and need experienced owners, so they do not become over dominant and difficult to handle.

- **Horses are gelded** from the age of about six months, so they cannot reproduce.

- **Geldings** are usually more dependable and tolerant than other horses.

- **If mares and geldings** are kept together at grass they may fight for dominance, each trying to be the leader of the group.

▼ *In the wild, stallions will normally have a harem of four or five mares. They will live together in a group with other animals made up of foals, yearlings, and some two-year-olds.*

Mares

- **A mare is** a mature female horse. A filly is a young female horse.

- **Mares are pregnant**, or "in foal," for 11 months. Most give birth to a single baby called a foal.

- **A mother**, or dam, recognizes her foal by smell. She spends the first hour after birth licking and sniffing her foal to create a bond between them.

- **Mares produce milk** for their young and will feed them for up to six months before they are weaned.

- **During foaling**, mares need peace and quiet. Disturbing them may cause their labor to stop. The most common time of year for a foal to be born is in spring.

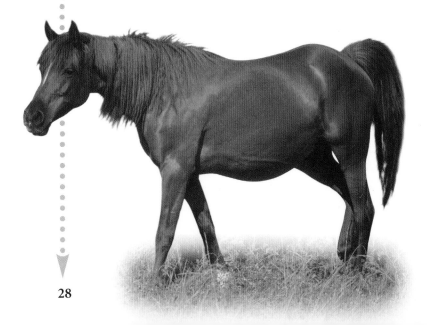

◀ *A pregnant mare has to carry the extra weight of a foal. She needs more food than usual to meet the nutritional requirements of her growing young.*

▶ *This mare is alert to danger as her head is held high and her ears are pricked. Her foal is ready to follow her lead if she decides they should run from danger.*

- **Mares should not** normally be ridden after they are five months pregnant.

- **A mare is said** to be in heat, receptive to a stallion and fertile, for about five days in every 21-day cycle.

- **Mares mainly come into heat** when the days are longest and warmest— from early spring until late fall. Although a mare becomes less fertile with age, she can often continue to produce offspring into her late teens.

- **Mares in heat** can be more sensitive than geldings. During this time some object to being brushed or having their girths tightened and require sensitive handling.

```
. . . FASCINATING FACT . . .
Some mares reject their foals. The foals
can sometimes be raised by a foster mare.
```

29

Foals

- **When foals are born** their legs are almost the same length as when they are fully-grown. Newborn foals cannot eat grass because their long legs prevent them from reaching it.

- **Spring is the usual** time for foals to be born, as the weather improves and grass is at its most nutritious for mares.

- **Foals can focus** their eyes almost as soon as they are born. Within an hour they can stand up and walk.

▲ *Shetland ponies grow thick manes and tails to protect them from the elements.*

- **Within a day** a foal can gallop to keep up with its mother.

- **A newborn foal** will often kick out if touched on its quarters by an animal other than its mother.

- **Foals tend to sleep** flat on the ground rather than standing up.

◀ *Young foals have very long legs in relation to their body. As they develop, their body proportions balance out.*

- **Foals like to play**, and enjoy chasing and grooming each other. In the wild, filly foals may stay with their mother for several years as part of a family group.

- **Foals cut** their first teeth within a week and have a full set of teeth by about nine months.

- **Foals start on solids**, picking at grass, or investigating their mother's feed buckets, from six weeks. They should be wormed for the first time at this stage.

- **A foal** is called a yearling after its first birthday. They are fully grown by three to four years of age.

▶ *A mare will continue to suckle a foal until it is about six months old. By this time the foal will be eating a variety of other foodstuffs and be ready for weaning.*

Herds

- **Horses are highly social** animals, preferring to live in family groups that join together into herds. This is called the herding instinct.

- **A herd is usually** led by a mare who decides when the group should move on to look for fresh grazing. She also maintains discipline.

- **In the wild**, one horse in the herd will always be on guard. If it senses danger, it will alert the others who will follow the leader, if necessary at speed. This is called the flight mechanism.

- **Horses are able** to run very quickly, reaching speeds of up to 30 mph (48 km/h) in four seconds or less. However, they are not designed to gallop for prolonged periods of time.

- **In the wild**, foals usually stay close to their mothers. When there is danger they are moved to the center of the group and protected by the adults.

▶ *In a herd, horses who bond, or get along well with each other, will groom and nuzzle one another and graze together.*

▲ *A lead mare determines how a wild herd reacts to any situation.*

● **Horses can** communicate with other members of the herd through both vocal and body signals.

● **Fighting with intent** to injure is uncommon as horses show their displeasure in a number of other ways: by lashing their tails, flattening their ears, or striking out with their front legs.

● **Domestic animals** often lack the company of an entire herd and can feel vulnerable. It is important to offer a horse some company, if not another horse then a donkey or sheep.

● **When a horse** is sold or dies, leaving another horse alone, the remaining animal will often grieve for its missing friend and can show signs of depression.

... FASCINATING FACT ...
In the wild, horses spend up to 70 percent of their time grazing.

Teeth

- **A horse has two sets** of teeth in its life. A foal has a set of milk (baby) teeth. These are worn down as it is weaned and begins to graze, and are replaced by the adult (permanent) teeth.

- **A horse's teeth** continue to grow from the root throughout its life. No new tooth is formed but the tooth beneath the gum line pushes upward.

- **By the age** of five, a horse will have all its permanent teeth. Horses have upper and lower incisors, so they can nip grass very short.

- **In old age**, from about 20 onward, a horse will begin to lose its molar teeth.

- **The maximum number** of teeth an adult male horse has is 44.

- **A dentist needs** to visit a horse at least once a year. The dentist rasps the horse's teeth with a special file. This is called floating. It ensures there are no sharp edges to the teeth, which could prove painful, cause ulcers, and stop the horse from eating.

- **Some horses dislike** dental treatment and have to be sedated.

▲ *The metal bit sits in the gap between a horse's incisors and premolar teeth.*

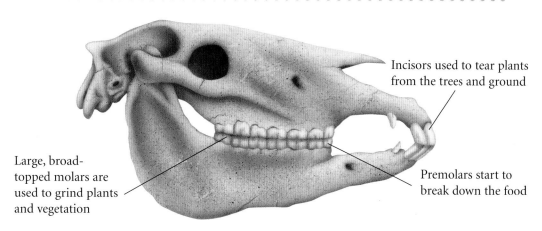

Incisors used to tear plants from the trees and ground

Large, broad-topped molars are used to grind plants and vegetation

Premolars start to break down the food

▲ *Different types of teeth are used in eating. The surface of the teeth is worn down by about 0.1 in (3 mm) every year.*

- **The best way** to discover the age of a horse is to examine its teeth. As a horse gets older, its incisors become worn down and protrude from its mouth. Vets can also tell a horse's age from changes and marks on the teeth.

- **A very old horse** will have very short molars. A molar might only be 1.1 in (3 cm) long compared to 3.1 in (8 cm) in a young horse.

. . . **FASCINATING FACT** . . .
There is a space between a horse's incisors and premolars. By inserting a thumb into this gap a horse can be encouraged to open its mouth.

Body facts

- **On average**, the stomach of a horse can hold about 2 to 3 gal (9 to 12 lt). Food passes through the digestive system quickly.

- **A horse** cannot vomit.

- **Horses need** to eat a lot of fiber or bulk foods, such as grass and hay. They need to consume about 2.5 percent of their bodyweight in dry matter each day.

- **Some ponies** don't know when to stop eating. This can cause colic and laminitis if their pasture is too lush.

- **Oils, such as vegetable**, soya, or linseed can be added to a horse's feed to help improve its coat condition and add extra calories to the diet.

- **After feeding**, horses produce manure or droppings. In a healthy horse, these should break softly when they hit the ground, being neither hard pellets nor liquid manure.

▶ *On average, a horse at grass eats for 15 out of every 24 hours.*

···FASCINATING FACT···
The oldest horse on record is Old Billy, who died in
November 1822 at the age of 62.

● **A horse drinks** at least 5.5 gal (25 lt) of water each day, about 13 times as much as an adult human.

● **The horse has** a particular way of smelling, known as the Flehmen response, which involves turning out its upper lip and extending his nose in the air.

● **Horses can suffer** from cracked lips. The sides of their mouths should be inspected regularly.

▲ *This horse is using the Flehmen response to assess an unusual smell or scent.*

Poisons

- **Apart from** the obvious dangers from chemicals and herbicides, which may be used or stored inappropriately, horses can easily poison themselves with the natural vegetation found in their fields, or in the trees and hedges surrounding their paddocks.

- **Horses are** more likely to be tempted to eat poisonous plants if kept hungry and on poor-quality grass. Care should be taken to ensure that poisonous plants are removed from within their reach.

- **Paddocks must be inspected** weekly as new seeds may germinate after the parent plant has been removed. A ragwort plant can produce 150,000 seeds.

- **All parts of yew**, *Taxus bacata*, can cause immediate death if ingested.

- **Eating ragweed**, a greenish flowering weed, affects the liver and can result in death.

▲ *In full flower, ragweed is easy to recognize. Horseowners must be vigilant in removing it from the environment of horses.*

- **The tree** *Laburnum vossii* has poisonous seeds and leaves that can leave a horse in a coma if eaten.

- **If poisoned** by eating bracken, *Pteridium*, a horse will grow increasingly sleepy and arch its back.

- **Even the common buttercup**, *Ranunculus*, is mildly poisonous and can cause mouth irritation. However, when dried in hay, it is quite safe.

- **Both acorns and oak leaves** are poisonous to horses. Trees in surrounding fields should be identified and if necessary prevent horses from gaining access to them. In the fall, windfall acorns and leaves should be removed in case they are blown into areas where horses graze.

▶ *Oak poisoning occurs after eating acorns and oak leaves. Death often occurs.*

> ...FASCINATING FACT...
> Horses should never be fed mown grass as
> it can cause serious colic.

Points and condition

- **A horse's body parts** are identified through a series of points. These recognized terms are used to pinpoint particular areas of the body.

- **Condition** refers to a horse's outward appearance of health. A shiny coat, clear eyes, clean nose, and ribs that can be felt but not seen, are all indicators of good condition.

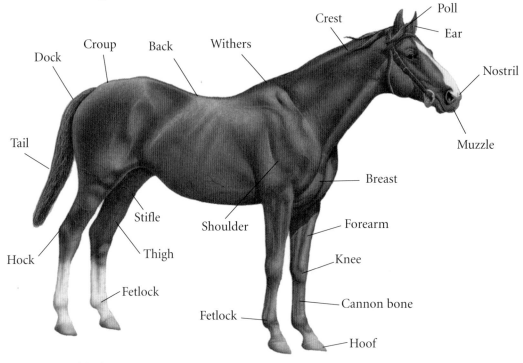

▲ *Points of the horse*

- **Worms that live** in a horse's system are parasites. If left undisturbed, they result in loss of condition and in cases of severe infestation, colic.

- **Regular worming** throughout the year is essential in domestic horses to keep infestation under control.

- **Laminitis is** a painful foot condition which restricts the blood flow to the feet. An affected horse will often stand, placing its weight on its heels, to relieve the pain.

- **A horse's temperament** cannot be quickly assessed. It is necessary to study a horse's behavior in relation to other horses, as well as its interaction with humans. This determines whether it is generally a quiet, dependable sort or an independent flighty animal.

- **Hocks are joints** on a horse's hind legs.

- **The withers should** be the highest point on a horse's back. They are found at the base of the mane.

- **Heels are found** on the underside of a horse's foot. A farrier must take care when shoeing that the shoe does not impinge on the heel, causing corns.

- **Fetlock joints** are found on all four legs. They are below the horse's knee on its front legs and below the hocks on its back legs.

Saddles

- **Saddles are a vital piece** of equestrian equipment. A good well-fitting saddle carries the rider in the correct position without causing the horse any discomfort.

- **Traditionally made** from leather, lighter synthetic saddles are now popular. They come in a variety of seat sizes to suit the rider and a number of different styles, such as pony, jumping, dressage, and general-purpose.

- **Saddles should be cleaned** and checked regularly to ensure the stitching is safe and there are no lumps forming underneath the seat that could damage the horse's back.

- **When buying a new saddle**, an experienced saddle fitter should fit one which is appropriate for both horse and rider.

- **As horses change shape** through losing or gaining fitness, the fit of a saddle should be reassessed regularly.

- **Numnahs are saddle-shaped** pads that sit underneath the saddle to protect the horse's back and should not be used to try to correct an ill-fitting saddle. They also help keep the saddle free from dirt and sweat.

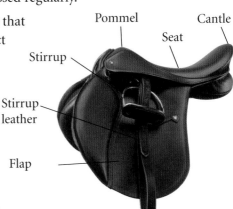

Pommel

Cantle

Seat

Stirrup

Stirrup leather

Flap

▶ *To ensure saddles are safe for use, the stitching, girth straps, and leathers should be regularly checked for wear and cracks.*

- **Girths secure a saddle** on the horse and come in a variety of shapes, materials, and designs, depending on the discipline. They must not rub the horse or damage the delicate skin around its middle.

◀ *A dressage saddle has a straighter cut and is slimmer fitting than a general-purpose saddle. This allows the rider a closer connection to the horse and an elongated leg position.*

- **Stirrup leathers** are the two leather loops suspended from a saddle that hold the metal foot rest, the stirrups, to support the rider's feet. Although traditionally referred to as "leathers," they are now also available in webbing and synthetic material.

- **Stirrup irons** should be big enough to allow about 0.5 in (1 cm) of clearance each side of the rider's boot.

Bridles

- **A bridle is headgear** used to control a horse's movement and direction and is a rider's primary means of communication with its head, mouth and nose.

- **Like saddles**, most bridles are made of leather but now also come in different materials such as webbing which has the advantage of being easily cleaned.

- **Bridles come** in three basic sizes: pony, cob, and full size. The pieces can be mixed and matched to suit each animal. They can be adjusted easily to ensure a good fit, and taken apart for cleaning.

- **A snaffle bridle** consists of several pieces that fit together: a headpiece, a throatlash, two cheek pieces, a brow band, a nose band, a pair of reins, and a snaffle bit.

▶ *The simplest form of English-style bridle is called a snaffle bridle.*

- **A bit is part** of a bridle that fits into a horse's mouth. Different styles of bit include the snaffle, the curb, and the Pelham.

- **Bits are made** in different materials, including metal and rubber, and in various sizes.

- **A correctly sized bit** should show 0.25 in (0.5 cm) either side of the horse's mouth to ensure it does not pinch its lips.

- **Some bridles are bitless**, such as the hackamore, and work by adding pressure on a horse's nose.

- **Whichever bridle is chosen**, it is important to keep it clean by regularly removing dirt and sweat, and cleaning the bit in running water after use. Well-maintained saddlery is vital for the comfort and safety of horse and rider and will help to ensure that the tack lasts.

- **Where a horse has** a particularly thick mane, it is common to remove a 1 in (2 cm) strip of mane to allow the bridle headpiece to fit tidily behind its ears.

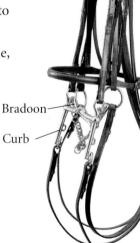

Bradoon

Curb

▶ *A double bridle has two metal bits, a bradoon (snaffle bit) and a curb bit, and two sets of reins. This type of bridle is used for showing and dressage and should only be used by experienced riders.*

Western tack

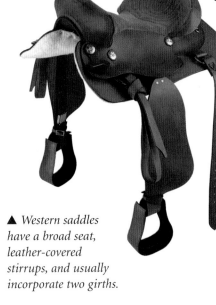

▲ *Western saddles have a broad seat, leather-covered stirrups, and usually incorporate two girths.*

● **Saddles used in** western-style riding are heavier than English saddles with a broader seat, spreading the rider's weight over as wide an area of the horse's back as possible. They are designed to be comfortable even if long hours are spent riding in them.

● **Western saddles** were developed from Spanish saddles. They were designed to carry a cowboy and all his gear.

● **The high horn** on western saddles was traditionally used as an aid to roping cattle.

● **The stirrup leathers** on a western saddle are called fenders.

● **The large western-type** stirrups are traditionally made from wood encased in leather.

● **The saddles** are made from leather. The show saddles, which are status symbols, are highly ornate, decorated with silver, and heavily patterned leather. There are also saddles specifically designed for leisure riding that are lighter.

- **Saddle blankets** are used to protect the horse's back. Cowboys often used them as bed rolls while cattle ranching.

- **The western-style bridle** differs from its English counterpart. It may have loops over either one or both ears and does not usually have a nose band.

- **Western bridle reins** are usually split into two distinct pieces. Each separate piece is held in one hand.

- **The famous American actor** John Wayne presented Queen Elizabeth II with the saddle he used in the making of the film, *The Alamo*.

◀ *The western saddle is built with practicality in mind. It is geared to the needs of the rider and the equipment needed for moving and catching cattle.*

Grooming kit

- **Every domestic horse** should have its own grooming kit that is kept solely for its own use. This prevents infectious skin conditions being passed to other animals. The kit keeps the horse clean and healthy and its feet free from stones.

- **The basic kit** consists of brushes, sponges, a hoof pick, and a means of cleaning the brushes. It is important to regularly remove dirt, hair, and old skin matter.

- **The dandy brush** is used to remove dried mud and dirt from a horse's winter coat. It has long, stiff bristles and is usually used on the less sensitive parts of the horse's body.

- **The body brush** is softer and is used to remove grease and dust from a horse's summer coat. It can be used on sensitive areas such as the head, stomach, or inside the legs.

- **A water brush** is used for applying water to the horse's coat, mane, and tail when dampening or washing.

- **A rubber or plastic curry comb** is used to remove dried mud and loose hair from the coat. A metal curry comb should never be used on a horse but is used to remove dust and dirt from the brushes.

- **Mane combs** are often metal, but sometimes plastic, and are used to comb the mane and tail of the horse.

- **Hoof picks** are used for removing dirt and stones packed into the underside of a horse's hoof. Hooves should be picked out daily.

● **Stable sponges** are ordinary foam sponges used for cleaning the eyes, nose, nuzzle, and tail area. A stable rubber or good linen tea towel can be dampened and gently wiped over the body to give the horse a final polish.

● **Where horseowners share** facilities, for example at a livery yard, each brush should be labeled with the owner's or horse's name. Grooming should be done outside so that dust is not inhaled. A lightweight plastic container or a canvas bag with drawstring top makes an excellent storage for a grooming kit.

▲ *An everyday grooming kit should contain items essential for keeping a horse clean.*

First-aid kit

- **There are a number** of essential first-aid items every horseowner should have in case of accidents or emergencies, but a vet must always be called if there is any doubt as to the severity of an injury or the welfare of a horse.

- **A basic kit should contain** commercial poulticing material that can draw out impurities from a wound. This is particularly useful if a horse suffers an abscess in the foot (see common ailments).

- **Wadding is useful** to remove dirt and to absorb blood from an injury. The wadding should have a layer that stops the dressing sticking to the wound. Cold running water is also useful to clean wounds and sooth bruising.

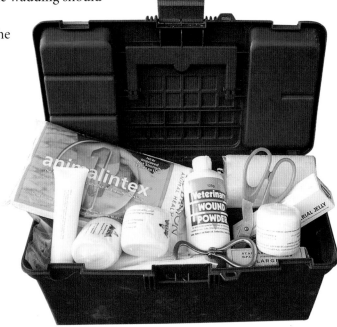

▶ *A first-aid kit for a horse should be clearly labeled. It should be kept out of reach of children in a clean, dry area.*

- **A rubber boot**, which can be securely attached to a foot over the shoe and hoof area, is a useful item and helps protect an injury.

- **Elastic bandages** for holding a poultice in place are essential, but care must be taken when applying wraps to ensure they are not tied too tightly. It is a good idea to practise bandaging a horse's foot or leg.

- **Access to cold water**, disinfected containers, sharp, clean scissors, and unused sponges should also be part of a basic kit.

- **A suitable antiseptic** for use on a horse's skin and a barrier cream to soothe sore skin and heels should be included.

- **Wound powder or gel** should be kept for minor abrasions.

- **A pair of tweezers** is useful in case a thorn or splinter has to be removed from an injury.

- **Cool gel packs** can be used on areas of strain or swelling to reduce inflammation.

Blankets

- **Domesticated animals**, who often have heavy winter coats removed, require protection against the elements.

- **There is a huge variety** of blankets available, in different sizes and materials, each with a different purpose. Each horse should have at least two blankets in case one is damaged or saturated with rain.

- **The most basic blanket** is one which simply keeps the rain off. These are useful for animals who do not need additional warmth but require protection from wet weather.

- **Fine-coated animals**, or those who have been clipped, need blankets that offer warmth as well as being waterproof. Blankets come in different weights with neck attachments to offer maximum protection.

- **Stable blankets are used** to provide warmth indoors but are not water-repellent. A lightweight cotton summer sheet can be used in warmer weather to keep the horse's coat clean.

◀ Daily decisions should be made as to whether it is necessary to blanket a horse, depending on the temperature and weather conditions

► *Stable blankets are available in different weights and styles. The blanket chosen should suit the season and temperature.*

- **Wicking blankets**, which allow moisture to escape, are useful in drying a horse that is wet from rain or sweat.

- **Traveling blankets protect** the horse from injury while on the move and shield it from cold drafts. Fly sheets keep insects off and protect a horse's coat from fading in the sun.

- **Part blankets or exercise sheets**, which sit behind the saddle, offer protection from the weather while a horse is exercising. Some have flashing lights attached to alert other road users of the horse's presence in dim light.

- **Whenever blankets are worn** they should be checked at least twice a day to ensure they are not rubbing the horse, particularly at shoulder level, and have not slipped when the horse has been lying down.

- **Blankets need to be cleaned** and mended before storing, to keep them in good condition.

Traveling equipment

- **Traveling in a horse trailer** is an unnatural experience for a horse and every effort should be made to make the journey as stress-free as possible.

- **The horse should wear** safety equipment to help prevent any injury to its body during loading, unloading, or traveling.

- **In order to lead** a horse into a trailer, the animal needs to be fitted with an appropriately sized headcollar and traveling rope.

- **An anxious horse** will often throw its head up high, so it is important to protect the vunerable poll area (between the horse's ears). A poll guard can be fitted to the headcollar to provide protection.

- **Traveling boots** fitted to each leg protect against injury. In addition, knee and hock defenders can be worn for extra protection.

- **A blanket is used to protect** the horse from drafts while traveling, but care should be taken to ensure that the blanket is not too warm as this could make the horse sweat and become uncomfortable.

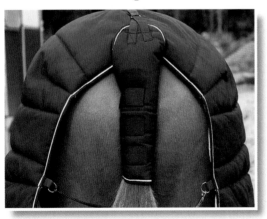

◀ *Tail guards help prevent damage to the horse's tail. The guard should not be secured too tightly as this may hinder circulation.*

- **A tail guard** prevents the tail being rubbed during traveling.

- **The person loading** the animal should be correctly dressed, in a hard hat and stout boots. Gloves should also be worn in case the leading rope is unexpectedly pulled through their hands.

- **If a haynet is left** with the horse while traveling, it must be secured at a height where the horse cannot paw at it and entangle itself in the net.

- **Any unsecured items** must be removed from the traveling area before setting off as these may move around and frighten or injure the animal.

▼ *Before traveling a horse, the owner should practice loading and unloading at home to familiarize the animal with the trailer.*

Rider wear

- **Someone riding** for the first time at a riding school needs very little equipment. Clothing should not be too tight or uncomfortable and possession of a pair of stout boots with a small heel is all that is necessary. Most riding schools are happy to provide safety hats for beginners.

- **Riding clothes are designed** to be practical and neat, but above all to give the rider protection in the event of an accident. A rider should always wear a protective hat that meets current safety standards.

- **Jodphurs or breeches** are comfortable and practical and protect the legs from being pinched or chaffed from stirrup leathers.

- **A body protector** provides protection for the back, neck, and shoulders, and is a good investment.

▶ *Long or short boots can be worn for general riding.*

▶ *An approved safety hat should always be worn for horseriding.*
A velvet-covered hat should be worn for competition riding.

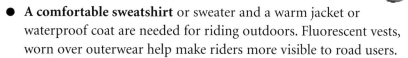

● **Short or full-length leather boots** with a clearly
defined heel give ankle support and prevent a
rider's foot slipping through the stirrup. Rubber
rain boots, while ideal for working in
the paddock, should not be worn for riding as
they may get caught in the stirrups.

● **A comfortable sweatshirt** or sweater and a warm jacket or
waterproof coat are needed for riding outdoors. Fluorescent vests,
worn over outerwear help make riders more visible to road users.

● **Gloves are essential**, both to keep hands warm and to prevent the reins
being pulled out of a rider's hands.

● **Long hair** should be neatly tied back.

● **Earrings** or any other form of jewelry should be removed before riding.

● **Riders wishing to take part** in competitive riding, such as showing,
jumping, or cross-country, will find there are dress codes for each
discipline which must be adhered to.

Road safety

- **When riding on roads** safety issues are very important for both horse, rider, and other road users.

- **If possible riders should always travel** with another rider, or a friend on a bicycle or walking alongside.

- **A young or inexperienced horse** should never be ridden on the road until it has proved itself in a controlled situation.

- **Riders should wear** high-visibility clothing to allow drivers the earliest chance of seeing them and driving with caution.

▲ *Even during the summer months when visibility is generally good, a rider wearing a fluorescent vest helps drivers to see them, particularly when moving into areas of shade on an otherwise bright road.*

- **A riding hat that meets** current safety standards should always be worn, together with a body protector.

- **Observation is one of the keys** to road safety. The rider should keep away from busy main roads and be alert to moving traffic, continually looking and listening for hazards that may alarm the horse.

- **Riders should give** clear and accurate signals to inform other road users where they are going.

- **Parked vehicles** should be given sufficient berth to allow a passenger to open a door without injuring the horse or rider.

- **Riders should inform** someone of their planned route and the time it will take them to complete it, so an alarm can be raised if they fail to return.

▲ *Horse and rider should be well prepared and wear suitable equipment for traveling on the road.*

- **A cellular phone should be carried** in order to call for help in the event of an emergency. Phones should be switched to silent mode while riding to avoid startling the horse with a ringing tone.

Happy and relaxed

- **A relaxed horse** allows its head and neck to hang low when at rest. A tense or anxious horse has its head held high, senses on full alert for danger.

- **A happy horse** may make chewing or licking movements with its mouth. This shows it is happy to do what its owner or another herd member wants and it does not want to fight or argue.

- **An excited or nervous horse** is said to be "on its toes"—ready to run off at any moment. A calm horse's walk will be unhurried.

- **A relaxed horse** may sigh or yawn and take deep breaths. A tense horse will have a rapid pulse, a rider may be able to feel its heart beating.

◀ *An alert expression denotes an animal that is healthy and happy.*

- **The skin should be soft** and supple, not stretched taut over the muscles.

- **The lips should be soft** and relaxed. The mouth should not be tight or pinched.

- **Eyes should be large** and clear. The membranes under the eyelids and linings of the nostrils should be salmon-pink in color.

- **The horse will be happy** to be touched all over and will show no sign of irritation, such as tail swishing.

- **The horse should offer** up a foot to be cleaned without hesitation on command. By freely giving a foot, the horse shows trust in its carer.

- **The horse will call out** and approach a familiar person if it sees them in its field, showing it is happy to be with them.

▲ *The eye of a horse should be clear without discharge running from it, which could indicate irritation or infection.*

61

Feeds and feeding

- **Horses have small stomachs** for their size and need to eat little and often. If kept in a field, horses will graze for most of the day. If forage is insufficient to meet the nutritional requirements of the horse, particularly those in work, additional feed may be needed.

- **Feed is one of the main costs** of keeping horses. However, feeding horses well-balanced diets is also the principal way of keeping horses healthy.

- **When choosing** a suitable diet for a horse, there are many different foodstuffs: concentrates, forage, supplements, vitamins, and herbs. However, grass is the most natural foodstuff and roughage must play the largest part in their diet.

- **Bought foodstuffs** fall into two basic categories: forage, such as hay and haylage, and concentrates, such as cereals, mixes, nuts, and pellets.

- **Whichever feeding regime** is chosen— depending on the type of horse, the season and the workload—it is essential to provide a balanced diet that contains correct levels of vitamins and minerals.

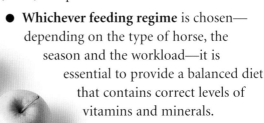

◀ *Succulents, such as apples and carrots, can be added to a feed ration to make it more appetizing.*

- **Proprietary balanced feeds** offer a consistent diet and are convenient to use. They are carefully formulated to meet the requirements of different types of horses and workloads, from high-fiber maintenance to high-energy performance rations.

- **All concentrates** should be kept in rodent-proof containers to avoid attracting vermin and wasting food. Hay should be stored off the ground in a dry, ventilated area.

- **Before purchase**, hay should be inspected to guarantee it is free from ragweed. It should not appear dusty, smell bad, or have any visible mold.

- **Sudden changes** in the type of food can cause digestive upset. All changes to the diet should be undertaken on a gradual basis.

- **Clean water** must be available at all times, either from a self-filling container or from a trough. In winter, water containers should be provided in frost-free areas to ensure the horse has a ready supply of water during cold weather.

Common ailments

- **COPD** (chronic obstructive pulmonary disorder) is an allergy commonly caused by dust or mold spores. It affects a horse's breathing and may result in a cough or nasal discharge. The horse should be seen by a vet. It is usually recommended that the horse spends as much time in the fresh air as possible, its stable is kept clean and dust free, and its hay is soaked in water so any dust or mould spores swell in size and are less easily inhaled.

- **Thrush** affects the underside of the hoof around the frog. It is often caused by unhygienic bedding or standing in wet muddy conditions. It can be identified by its foul smell.

- **An abscess** on the sole of the foot can produce dramatic lameness in a horse. It is a common problem often caused by small puncture wounds that allow infection to enter the foot. The abscess is usually drained and poulticed to draw out any remaining infection.

- **Horses can go lame** for a variety of reasons and it is usually detected in one of two ways. If the horse is lame in a front leg, it will raise its head as the sore leg hits the ground. Lameness in hind legs is harder to establish, but will show in unevenness in a horse's hip when being trotted.

- **Ear mites** cause irritation. An affected horse might shake its head and try to scratch its ears. The condition can be treated with creams.

- **Aural plaques** are wart-like flakes in the ears and are usually harmless.

- **Colic is abdominal pain** – it can usually be detected if a horse is looking agitated and uncomfortable, kicking at its stomach and trying to roll. Swollen patches may also appear over its body. Veterinary advice and treatment are essential as it is a potentially fatal illness.

▶ *Mud fever affects a horse's heels and lower legs and shows as sore, reddened, scabbed skin.*

- **Lice live on horses**, causing bald patches as the horse tries to itch the affected areas, and can be transferred by grooming with another horse's brush. Louse powders and shampoos are used to treat the problem.

- **Mud fever** is usually caused by standing in wet and muddy fields. Bacteria enter the softened skin around the legs and needs to be treated with special anti-bacterial washes and creams.

- **Laminitis** is inflammation of the sensitive laminae in a horse's foot and is very painful. It is likely to occur if a pony grazes for too long on overly lush or fresh grass. A horse might lie down or stand with its weight on its heels in an attempt to ease the pain. The hooves will feel warm when touched and a vet needs to be called immediately.

Worming

- **All horses have parasites** in their stomach and intestines. If they are there in small quantities, the effect on the horse will be barely noticeable. Danger arises when the parasite count builds up. The parasites form a continuous circle. Worm eggs are passed out of a horse in its droppings onto land used for pasture. As other horses graze, they pick up the larvae and swallow them. The worms then hatch out and live on the food that should be nourishing the horse.

- **A badly infested horse** can suffer from a number of related problems. It may lose condition and look thin, and have bouts of anemia or colic.

- **A horse owner** should carry out a regular program of worming throughout the year. There are several types of worm found in horses: red worms, tapeworms, lungworm, pin worms, round worms, and bots.

- **Worming products** can be bought from the vet or an authorized retail outlet, which will advise on a worming program, products available, and the amount required for the size of horse or pony.

- **Most horses** should be wormed every eight to ten weeks. All horses living together should be wormed at the same time.

- **Horses with** unknown worming history or who are new to a paddock should be wormed and kept apart from other horses for 48 to 72 hours: the amount of time it takes for food to pass through their system.

- **All droppings** should be removed from fields at least two or three times a week, and should be stored on a manure heap. The contents of a manure heap should not be spread over horse pasture.

- **Grazing horses** with sheep and cattle helps to keep worm levels down. The larvae do not affect sheep and cattle and die in their stomachs.

▶ *Paste wormers come in a syringe which is squeezed onto the horse's tongue.*

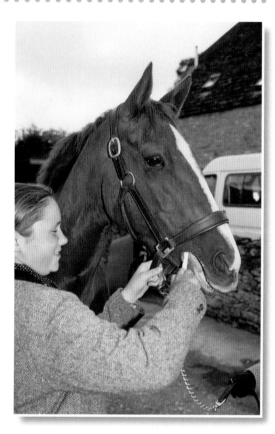

● **Wormers come in liquid**, powder, and paste forms. The liquid and powder varieties can be added to a horse's feed.

● **If a horse dislikes** having the syringe put into its mouth, it is important to work on the problem in advance of worming. Using a clean, empty syringe, accustom the horse to the look of it simply by placing it near its food, then begin touching him with it around the face and lips. If it objects, the syringe can be dipped in syrup until the horse is happy to have it placed in its mouth.

Horseshoes

- **People have** protected horses' feet with shoes for over 2,000 years.

- **A horse's feet** should preferably be cleaned out twice a day to ensure there are no stones, sticks, or mud trapped under the foot that could lead to lameness.

▲ *A hoof pick for cleaning horses' feet is a vital piece of equipment for every horseowner.*

- **Not all horseshoes** are nailed on. In special circumstances, plastic shoes can be glued on.

- **Racehorses wear** special lightweight shoes made of aluminum rather than the typical iron shoe. These are called racing plates.

- **Farriers have** been part of an organization in Britain since 1356, when the Worshipful Company of Farriers was formed.

- **Today**, farriers have to undergo extensive training to qualify as a registered farrier.

▶ *The pointed end of the anvil allows the farrier to shape a shoe to the correct size.*

◀ *After removing an old set of shoes, a farrier has to trim and balance the horse's feet prior to re-shoeing. He uses a rasp and special trimming knives.*

- **A farrier's job** is highly skilled. It requires knowledge not only of how to make and put on shoes, but also of the horse's movement and diseases of the foot.

- **Shoes can be fitted** by the farrier at the forge, or from a portable forge, which enables the farrier to travel to clients.

- **Special hardened studs** are sometimes added to shoes for better grip. There are types of stud for different ground conditions and disciplines.

> ... FASCINATING FACT ...
> The Romans used a type of iron sandal
> on their horses' feet.

Buying a horse

- **Horses and ponies** can be bought and sold in a variety of ways: by personal introduction, from a dealer, by advertisement, and at auction.

- **Before purchase**, it is important to find out as much as possible about the horse's history and ability. It is also important to consider its age, size, temperament, and conformation. A responsible seller should be able to produce a feeding program and veterinary and worming records.

- **An animal's price** will vary according to its type, age, experience, and quality. However, all horses and ponies should be vetted prior to purchase by an equine veterinary surgeon. During the vetting, the health and suitability will be examined and assessed.

▲ *A companion pony might be relatively cheap to buy, but will need the same standard of vet and farrier care as other horses.*

- **Blood tests and X-rays** can also be part of the vetting procedure.

- **Horses take time** to settle into new homes and may show atypical behavior for the first weeks after a move, such as wood chewing or box walking, while they adapt to their new surroundings, horses, and owner.

- **Horses require** twice-daily attention and year-round care. Anyone considering the purchase of a horse must be prepared and fully aware of the costs and time involved.

- **The purchase price** is only a small part of the cost of keeping the animal, which will include grazing, stabling, vetting, feeding, worming, tack, and insurance.

- **Although many horses** can and will live alone, they are herd animals by nature and thrive on company. When buying a horse or pony, it is worth considering providing it with a companion. Horses that are no longer suitable for riding, either because of age or disability, will be advertised for sale on this basis.

- **Horses are sometimes sold** with tack. Always check it to ensure that it does not cause any problems, and that it is in a safe condition and does not need to be restitched or reflocked.

- **When it is time to sell** a horse it is important to ensure its owner can load it into a trailer without upset, so that the move is as gentle as possible. This may require several weeks' practice in advance.

▶ *Before buying a horse determine whether the price includes tack and equipment.*

71

Stabling

- **Stables are used** to shelter a horse from the extremes of weather.

- **An average-sized stable** is 12 x 12 ft (3.7 x 3.7 m).

- **A stable should be built** with its back to the prevailing wind on level ground with a paved area to the front. If left as grass, this ground will quickly become churned up in wet weather.

- **The stable** and its doors should be of adequate height so the horse does not bang its head.

- **The stable must** have good ventilation to ensure the air inside does not become stale.

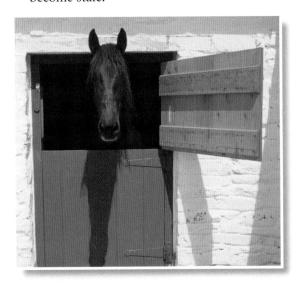

- **An overhang** at the front of the stable provides shade and protection from wind and rain.

- **The floor** of the stable should be non-slippery and hard-wearing. Concrete with rubber matting is often used as it can be washed down and disinfected easily.

▲ *The stable door should be high enough for the horse to easily walk through without banging its head. This door height is too low the horse.*

- **Stable doors** are usually divided in two halves, so the top part can be fastened back and the stabled horse can see out and have access to fresh air. The doorway should be wide enough to allow the horse to pass through it comfortably. The top edge of the bottom door should be protected by a metal strip to stop the horse from chewing it.

- **Stables should be** cleaned out regularly, and droppings and wet material removed daily.

- **Horses kept** in stables for long periods without any form of exercise can develop behavioral problems such as weaving, crib-biting, windsucking, and box walking (see behavioral problems).

▲ *Horses are well-protected from rain and wind by the overhang on these stables. They also allow horses to see their companions.*

Field shelters and barns

- **All horses** and ponies kept at grass require an effective field shelter. They not only require protection from the cold, wet, and windy weather, but need shade during the summer to provide shade and protection from flies.

- **Field shelters** are usually open-fronted sheds that may house just one or several horses. They are sited in the paddock so that horses choose when to use them.

▼ *A field shelter or open barn offers protection from the elements.*

- **The size of the shelter** will depend on the number of horses and ponies that will use it at any one time, and on its shape.

- **It is increasingly believed** that horses should have as much free time at grass in the company of others as possible. This might mean only bringing a horse into its stable for warmth and safety at night, allowing several horses to share an open barn, or leaving horses free to choose whether to use the field shelter in their paddock.

- **Shelters may be** sited directly onto the ground but still need to be cleaned of droppings regularly.

- **Mobile field shelters** are designed to allow for movement between paddocks. They provide a versatile and convenient option where different areas of grazing are used.

- **Horses can share** a large barn at night or in bad weather. Often a deep bed of straw is used in a barn and it is cleaned out mechanically once or twice a year.

- **Communal living** means that horses don't get lonely and can stand together for comfort and warmth.

- **One of the disadvantages** of allowing several horses to share a field shelter or barn is that infection can spread quickly and a newcomer might be picked on by others.

- **A horse** with a dust allergy may be unsuitable for communal living. If it has to have dust-free bedding it will need separate accommodation.

Paddocks

- **Domesticated horses** have only a limited area of grass in which to eat, play, socialize and leave their droppings. Each horse needs about 1 to 1.5 acres of grazing.

- **A horse's carer** is responsible for the management of the paddock. This involves removing droppings regularly, checking for and removing any poisonous plants, and filling in any holes a horse could stumble into. Garbage should also be removed daily.

- **The border fencing** and hedging around a paddock must be well maintained to ensure horses cannot escape or injure themselves. It should be 3ft 6 in to 4 ft 6 in (1 to 1.4 m) high. Barbed or thin wire fencing should be avoided.

- **In spring and early summer** and again in late fall when the grass is growing quickly, it might be necessary to restrict grazing, particularly where lush grazing could result in laminitis or colic. Electric fencing is useful where temporary barriers are needed to contain horses.

- **Winter brings** a different set of problems for the horseowner, as rain and snow can rapidly turn a paddock into sodden mud. Areas of wet, churned mud often develop around areas of heaviest use, such as food and water areas, gateways, and stable entrances.

- **If enough grazing is available**, it is a good idea to divide it into smaller sections. This allows one area to be grazed while the other sections rest. If possible, the wettest area should be taken out of use in winter.

- **A wet field** can result in horses developing ailments such as mud fever or thrush. To help alleviate these potential problems, paved or gravel areas should be provided and long-term drainage solutions sought.

- **Entrance gates** should be wide enough to lead a horse through without risk of injury. Good maintenance is necessary to ensure the horse is not in danger from sharp edges or broken panels.

- **Horses should always have** access to fresh water. A trough should be provided in the field that can be checked daily and refilled as necessary.

- **A horse's pasture** must be kept under control as horses are selective grazers and will leave areas of weeds such as plantains, dock, thistles, and nettles, concentrating on more tasty grass. This results in areas of rough grass, while other areas are grazed down to the ground. If weeds are ignored, they will gradually spread, reducing the amount of pasture available to the horse.

▶ *Turnout headcollars with quick release straps should be used in the field. They are specially designed to pull free if the horse becomes caught on fencing.*

Hints and tips

- **Keeping a horse** is expensive and time-consuming. It should be a source of pleasure, but an unwell animal is a cause for concern and is likely to incur vet bills. It is therefore important to be aware of your horse's condition and to take action before any problems develop.

- **Insurance policies** are available to cover third-party liability, loss-of-use, and veterinary treatment and costs.

- **Share the responsibility** of horse care with other horseowners, so that you can look after each other's horses rather than having to pay someone else to do it.

▶ *Muddy conditions encourage mud fever. To help avoid this, make a paved or gravel area at gateways.*

- **Get together** with others to buy in bulk. Savings can often be made by buying large quantities of various products.

- **Develop a routine** for essential daily chores to save time and energy.

- **Be prepared to be flexible** in your choice of horse blankets and equipment. Last year's color or design may be reduced by the retailer, but still be of excellent quality.

- **Try to source** your hay and straw locally, so that you do not have to pay large delivery charges.

- **Keep a spare pair** of overalls and boots in the tack room so clothes do not get dirty when visiting a horse in its field.

- **Book regular appointments** with the farrier for re-shoeing every six weeks.

- **Take blankets** to be cleaned and repaired as soon as winter is over in order to keep them in good condition.

▶ *Store all emergency numbers, such as the vet, farrier, and doctor, in your cellphone.*

Horse whispering

- **Horse whispering has moved** from folklore to established practice.

- **People now understand** and appreciate it is a means of communicating in the way a horse naturally understands.

- **Horses have a range** of ways of communicating with each other. This range spans vocalizing with neighs and whickers, minor visual signs, such as flicking an ear or clamping down a tail, to posturing, such as striking out with a leg or rearing, and body stances that can indicate submission or dominance.

- **By learning "horse language,"** problems can be sorted out more effectively. By understanding that the horse is a flight animal who will run away from perceived danger the trainer can begin to work out how best to deal with the horse.

- **If a horse is approached** directly by a person who is square on and looking it directly in the eye, the horse will see this as someone who is confrontational, and may flee. The person should stand still, eyes averted, in a welcoming posture with a shoulder dipped in the direction of the horse. The horse might then feel able to approach. If it is not interested, the person can walk in large arcs backward and forward toward the horse and possibly be accepted.

- **Horses have basic signs** of submission, such as licking and chewing and dropping the head down low. A horse showing such signs does not want to go against the herd leader, which could be a human.

- **Horses move each other on** by walking behind another horse's flanks and possibly nudging them with their noses. A human can also move a horse in this way by walking behind and slightly to the side of the horse.

- **Horses have a natural fear** of many things. Humans cannot expect them not to be afraid but they can be trained not to run away, to trust their carer, and accept that they will not be put in any real danger.

- **Many horse communicators** use special halters. These make it easier for the handler to teach the horse the difference between acceptable and unacceptable behavior.

- **Monty Roberts is a leading** US exponent of horse whispering and has done much to establish it around the world.

▶ *Horses often form a strong relationship with another horse they live with—this is called pair-bonding. These horses have closer relationships with each other than with other horses in their field.*

The healthy horse

▲ *A healthy horse's general appearance is one of well-being. It will appear relaxed and content in the paddock.*

- **When looking after a horse**, it is important to be aware of what is "normal" for the individual. If a horse is behaving unusually, its carer is quickly aware of the situation and can act promptly.

- **A healthy horse** has bright clear eyes, which are not weeping or discharging down its nose. The ears should be alert, not drooping or uninterested or held tightly back.

- **The normal temperature** of a horse is 99.5 to 101.3°F (37.5 to 38.5°C).

- **Respiration at rest** should be between 10 to 20 inhalations a minute.

- **A horse's pulse** rate is normally 35 to 45 heart beats a minute at rest.

- **The coat** should be supple and shiny, not dull.

▶ *Much can be surmized about a horse's health simply by taking a good look at its demeanor and expression. An interested expression suggests the horse is not unwell or in distress.*

- **A healthy horse supports** its weight on all four feet equally and shows no sign of swelling or heat in its feet or legs.

- **The sounds** coming from a horse's stomach should be "normal" for that individual and not particularly loud. The stomach should not be distended and the horse should be eating and drinking normally.

- **The tail** should be relaxed and not clamped down between the horse's back legs.

- **A horse should not stand** in a depressed manner at the back of its stable or away from companions in the paddock. Any signs of irritable or atypical behavior may indicate the horse is feeling unwell.

Behavioral problems

- **Behavioral problems or vices** can be the result of stress or boredom. If a horse is confined in a stable alone over long periods of time, it will become unhappy and will often develop unwelcome habits. The solution is often to turn out the horse for longer periods and in the company of other horses.

- **Weaving** occurs when a horse stands at an open stable door repeatedly swinging its head from one side to another. Boxwalking is a pattern of behavior where the horse refuses to settle and walks repeatedly around the confines of its stable.

- **Crib-biting** is the habit of biting or chewing wood. Considerable damage can be caused to gates, fencing, and stables.

- **Windsucking** is similar to crib-biting, the horse attaches its teeth to a piece of wood and sucks in air.

- **If a horse starts to misbehave** when ridden, it may not be bad behavior, especially if the behavior is unusual, but a response to pain.

- **If a horse begins to buck**, particularly when asked to canter, the problem may lie with the saddle that should be checked immediately.

- **If a horse begins to headshake**, this may indicate a tooth problem and a professional horse dentist should examine its teeth.

- **If a horse shows reluctance** to be saddled, the saddle should be checked immediately. Massaging the back and stretching might be helpful, particularly for an older horse.

- **If after checking** the tack and consulting professionals the horse's behavior is still poor or dangerous, it may require further schooling to ensure it understands and obeys basic aids.

- **The rider** may also benefit from further riding lessons to ensure aids are being given correctly and that they are not putting themselves in any danger from the horse.

▲ *A rearing horse is dangerous for any rider. Immediate action should be taken to find and remove the cause.*

Daily routine

- **Horses enjoy routine** and expect to be fed at roughly the same time every day. A horse will be more restless if its carer is inconsistent.

- **A horse** should be visited every morning to check it is safe and well.

- **During the morning visit**, the horse should be fed, if necessary, its feet picked out, and any blankets adjusted. It may be possible to remove a field blanket during the day if the weather is mild and this will allow the horse the enjoyment of a roll in the dirt. Plenty of fresh water should always be available in the stable or field.

- **Manure should be removed** from the field. The stable or shelter should be cleaned and prepared for the evening.

- **If a horse is to be ridden**, at least an hour should be allowed after feeding for it to digest its food.

- **Grooming after exercise** is relaxing for the horse.

- **After riding**, a horse should have its feet picked out again and its blanket replaced, if necessary, before being returned to its field or stable. The tack should be inspected and cleaned.

- **In the evening**, the horse should be brought back inside if stabled, or checked again in the field. After feeding, feet and blanket checks should be carried out.

- **The feed buckets** should be cleaned out ready for the next feed.

- **The food and bedding supplies** should be checked and reordered regularly. The worming and vaccination program should also be checked to ensure it is being adhered to.

▼ *Blankets should be added or removed according to daily conditions.*

Grooming

- **A carer should be properly dressed** for dealing with horses, wearing gloves, stout boots, and, if necessary, a riding hat.

- **A headcollar and leading rope** should be put on the horse before bringing it out of its stable or field.

- **The horse should be tied up** using a slip knot that can be easily undone if necessary. Any blankets should be removed. If it is very cold, blankets can be turned over on themselves, leaving only a part of the horse's body exposed. This is known as quartering.

- **Grooming should begin** with picking out the feet. Mud, stones, and dirt should be removed so that the horse does not pick them up in its hooves again.

Dandy brush

- **The next stage** is to remove any mud or dirt from the horse's coat. In winter, a rubber curry comb and dandy brush will remove dried mud, but if the horse is kept outdoors, care should be taken not to overgroom, as natural grease in a horse's coat helps to keep it warm and dry.

Body brush

▲ *Different types of grooming brush can be used during a grooming session. Grooming stimulates circulation and helps keep the coat and skin clean and healthy.*

- **During summer**, on clipped horses or on sensitive areas of the body, a soft body brush should be used. The face should cleaned using a soft brush and sponge. It is best to untie the horse while cleaning this area, holding onto the leading rope with one hand.

- **Particular care** should be taken to thoroughly groom the areas where tack sits.

- **Brushes should be cleaned** repeatedly against a metal curry comb during the course of grooming.

- **A thorough grooming**, massaging the skin, removes dirt from the coat and makes the horse look clean and shiny. Once the neck and body are finished, including the legs, the mane and tail should be carefully brushed out.

- **While grooming**, never sit or kneel down next to the horse. Always squat, in case the horse is startled and moves suddenly.

▶ *A horse or pony should be happy to be touched all over, and should stand still, without fidgeting, while being groomed.*

Tacking up

- **A horse should be clean** prior to being tacked up. It should be approached in a calm manner. The bridle should be secured over one shoulder and the saddle carried over one arm with the girth looped over it. The stirrups should be positioned at the top of the stirrup leathers.

- **The underside of the saddle** should be checked by running a hand over it and any saddleblanket, to ensure there are no sharp objects or insects.

▼ *The rider should stand close to the horse while tacking up, using calm unhurried movements. Time should be taken to check that there are no twisted straps and that the saddleblanket is not creased or folded over.*

- **The rider should stand** on the horse's left-hand side. The saddle should be positioned on top of the saddleblanket and slid back into the correct place. The saddleblanket should be drawn well up into the gullet of the saddle to ensure that it does not press down onto the horse's withers.

- **The saddle should sit** far enough back to allow free movement of the horse's shoulders.

- **The rider should walk** around the front of the horse to drop the girth down from the saddle, then return to the left-hand side to fasten the girth so that the saddle is secure.

- **To put on the bridle**, the rider should stand to the horse's left alongside its head. The reins are then passed over the horse's head.

- **The bit is introduced** to the horse's mouth by inserting a thumb into the gap in its teeth, which helps to open the mouth and place the nose through the noseband.

- **The headpiece** is then fitted over the ears, the throatlash fastened and the noseband done up. Finally, a check should be made that no pieces of the bridle have been tangled and that the horse's forelock is lying tidily over the browband.

- **The rider** should then recheck the girth and tighten if necessary. The girth buckle guards should be pulled down and the horse's front legs stretched forward to ensure that there is no skin trapped beneath the girth.

- **Horses should not be left** tacked up for any length of time as they might try to roll, injuring their backs and possibly breaking the saddle.

Learning to ride

- **Riding schools should be** checked out by visiting them rather than simply booking a lesson by telephone.

- **When visiting a riding school**, a new customer should determine how the animals look, the condition of the stables and fields, and the facilities the school has to offer, for example indoor and outdoor arenas, floodlit areas, cross-country jumps, and hacking.

- **Beginners can expect** to be provided with riding hats. They will be introduced to a suitably sized, calm mount and shown how to get onto the horse.

- **The first lesson** will probably be conducted on a leading rein with a competent adult walking alongside the horse.

- **The rider will be taught** how to approach a horse correctly, how to mount and dismount, sit correctly, and how to hold the reins.

- **A new rider will master** the basics of balance and stability in the saddle, so that they do not injure the horse's mouth or back.

- **Children will gain confidence** as the riding instructor introduces fun movements into the sessions. They will be expected to take their feet out of the stirrups and "go around the world" on their ponies, turning to face the pony's tail and side, or lie back on their pony's back and touch its tail.

- **Rising trot** will be taught so that the rider feels the movement of the horse underneath and learns to "post" or rise in time with the stride.

- **Canter should be introduced** later when the rider has a confident seat and is able to control the speed and direction of the horse.

- **Jumping is taught** when the rider is proficient at all the basics of controlling speed, turning, and stopping and has a good balanced seat and hands that do not interfere with the horse's mouth.

▶ *Private one-to-one lessons are sometimes preferred by adults, but children usually enjoy the company and competitiveness of others.*

93

Welfare organizations

- **All domestic animals deserve** to be well-treated. Equine welfare organizations work toward protecting all horses, ponies, and donkeys.

- **The International League** for the Protection of Horses (ILPH) was set up in England in 1927 by Ada Cole. The main aim was to "prevent the ill-treatment of horses exported to Europe for slaughter."

- **The ILPH organization** is now one of the world's leading equine welfare charities and works to help horseowners and relieve suffering in animals.

- **In Britain**, the ILPH has four rehabilitation and recovery centers caring for about 300 horses.

▲ *International and national charities and organizations work worldwide to protect the best interests of horses, donkeys, and mules.*

- **In the USA**, as in Britain, there is legislation to protect horses. If someone is convicted of a serious offense against a horse they can be sent to prison and fined.

- **There are laws** that relate to performing animals, and those that regulate accommodation, pasture, and horses' welfare in riding schools.

- **Farriers are bound by laws** that aim to ensure horses are not subjected to unnecessary suffering by being shod by unskilled people.

- **The Brooke Hospital for Animals** is an international charity that aims to improve the working conditions of horses, donkeys, and mules. It offers education and training to owners who rely on these animals to make a living.

- **The Donkey Sanctuary** in England was set up 30 years ago by Dr Elisabeth Svendsen and has cared for almost 9000 donkeys.

- **The International Donkey Protection Trust** was also established by Dr Svendsen and works worldwide to improve conditions for working donkeys and mules in Europe, Africa, Egypt, India and Mexico.

▲ *Ponies living wild need to be monitored to make sure they are healthy. Welfare charities offer support and advice for owners and can take action if animals are in poor condition.*

Complementary therapy

- **Before any form** of complementary treatment is administered to a horse, a vet should be consulted for diagnosis of the problem and advice sought on such treatments.

- **In Britain**, the only forms of complementary treatment that can be given to animals by non-veterinary practitioners are manipulative treatments, such as chiropracty, osteopathy, and physiotherapy.

- **Osteopaths and chiropractors** work to reduce pain and increase mobility by manipulating the horse with their hands.

- **Physiotherapists** use their hands on the horse, but may incorporate other means such as hydrotherapy and ultrasound.

- **Hydrotherapy involves horses** walking into specially designed tanks in which they can swim. This exercise improves their muscles and builds up fitness without the animal having to support their own weight.

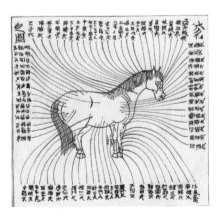

- **Acupuncture was brought** to Europe from China and can only be administered to horses by vets. Using special acupuncture needles on points around the body, the aim is to restore an animal's health by correcting its energy flow.

◀ *Acupuncture is an ancient treatment and is said to be able to help horses who suffer with a variety of common ailments.*

- **Some** holistic vets use aromatherapy and homeopathy to treat animals.

- **Equine sports massage** aims to encourage a quicker recovery after muscle damage occurs and is used frequently on competition horses.

- **Shiatsu** is a form of massage that is said to help both a horse's physical and mental state. It uses finger and palm pressure to stimulate a horse's natural healing ability.

- **A more controversial therapy**, which has claimed success in some cases, is distance healing. This usually involves sending a piece of horse's mane or tail to a healer who does not actually visit the horse, but thinks about it from a distance.

▼ *Swimming is especially helpful for horses who have limb problems. The water resistance means their muscles and heart have to work harder than on land, but they are at no risk from striking their legs on the ground.*

Arab

- **The Arabian Horse**, or Arab, is the oldest pure-bred horse in the world. Its head is small, with a dished face, large eyes, and a thin muzzle.

- **The Arab** was the horse of the Bedouin people—nomadic Arabs— as early as 3000 to 2500BC. They were later introduced into Europe.

- **This ancient breed** is widely regarded as the definition of beauty and elegance in horses. Famed for its speed, strength, and endurance, the Arab has influenced the development of almost all modern horse breeds.

- **Arabs** usually stand 14 hh to 15.2 hh.

- **Arabs are intelligent**, sensitive, and courageous creatures. They are also loyal, if well-treated, and enjoy attention.

- **Among the horses** that carried their famous riders into battle were Napoleon's Marengo, Alexander the Great's Bucephalus, and the Duke of Wellington's Copenhagen.

- **The earliest Arab horse** brought to the US was a stallion called Ranger, which arrived in 1765. It is said to have sired the horse George Washington rode during the American Revolutionary War.

◀ *The Arab has been used to improve the stock of other horse breeds throughout history. An Anglo-Arab is a cross between a Thoroughbred and a pure-bred Arab.*

▲ *At rest, an Arab horse's tail may trail on the ground, but when in action the tail is held high in the air.*

- **The action** of the Arab is unique and the breed is characterized by a "floating" movement—covering the maximum amount of ground with the minimum of effort.

- **During the Crimean War** (1851–54), one Arab horse raced 93 mi (153 km) without harm, but its rider died from exhaustion.

> **...FASCINATING FACT...**
> The Arab horse has 17 ribs—
> one less than other breeds.

Quarter Horse

▼ *The agility and speed of the Quarter Horse makes it ideal for ranch work.*

- **The breed** got its name because it was bred to race short distances—no more than a quarter of a mile. It is is the oldest all-American breed.

- **Quarter Horses** measure between 14 hh to 16 hh. They may be any whole color, but are mainly chestnut.

- **Powerful and muscular** conformation gives the Quarter Horse speed, ability, and balance.

- **The breed** was developed by English colonists in the early 1600s.

- **Known for** its "cow sense"—the ability to outmaneuver cattle—and calm disposition, the Quarter Horse was ideally suited for the challenge of the West.

- **The breed** is renowned for its versatility and excellent temperament.

- **The Quarter Horses is North America's** favorite breed with over two million listed by the American Quarter Horse Association and another 800,000 members worldwide.

- **The American Quarter Horse Association** was formed in 1940.

- **Quarter Horses** are used in western riding competitions, demonstrations, and rodeo.

> **...FASCINATING FACT...**
> Peter McCue, born in 1895 in Illinois, is the most famous breed stallion, credited with establishing the modern Quarter Horse.

Thoroughbred

- **The Thoroughbred** horse stands 15 hh to 16.2 hh.

- **The history** of the Thoroughbred and the birth of the racing industry are interlinked.

- **The introduction** of Arab blood increased the speed and endurance of the breed. They are now the most famous racehorses in the world.

- **Racing is called** "The Sport of Kings" because it was the English kings of the 15th century who encouraged the development of racing and breeding of Thoroughbreds.

▲ *Thoroughbred racing is popular sport. Different levels and lengths of race are held worldwide.*

- **The first Thoroughbred** arrived in America in 1730.

- **Thoroughbreds are usually whole colors**, especially bay, chestnut, and brown and often gray, black, and roan. Many have white markings.

- **Three famous stallions**, Byerley Turk, the Darley Arabian, and the Godolphin Arab are seen as the founders of the Thoroughbred breed.

- **Thoroughbreds are often unsuited** to inexperienced riders as they can be temperamental and may overreact to events. Horse that retire from the racing industry require careful rehabilitation and rehoming, but can be successful hunters and three-day eventers.

> ...**FASCINATING FACT**...
> Thoroughbreds can begin their racing
> career at just two years old.

● **Thoroughbreds** are often crossed with other breeds. These half- or part-bred animals make excellent competition horses in both the showing and showjumping world. Their influence has been used to improve breeds throughout the world.

▶ *The initials TB stand for Thoroughbred, while the term half-bred describes a horse who has only one parent that is a Thoroughbred.*

Shire and Clydesdale

- **One of the largest horses** in the world, the Shire, originated in England and is a descendant of the Old English Black Horse whose ancestors were the great horses of medieval times.

- **The Shire stands up to** 18 hh, and may be bay, brown, black, or gray.

- **Shires still work** the land in some parts of Britain and several brewers use them to pull drays in the city streets.

- **Shire numbers** dropped into the thousands after World War II but today there is a renewed interest in the breed. They are used as draft horses and bred with Thoroughbreds to make heavyweight hunters.

- **The Shire Horse Society** was founded in 1878 to "promote the old English breed of cart horse."

- **Clydesdales** are a breed of heavy draft horse, recognized for their strength, style, and versatility. The breed originated from Scottish farm horses over 200 years ago.

◀ *The mane and tails are ornately decorated for showing classes.*

- **Clydesdales** were not only used as pulling power on farms, but also transported goods within and between towns. They can pull many times more than their own weight, which is why the breed was so popular for transporting goods by wagon.

- **Clydesdales** can grow to over 18 hh. They are usually bay or brown in color with four white legs and a mass of soft feathers about the feet.

- **The Clydesdale** was the first draft horse in Great Britain to have an individual society. The Clydesdale Horse Society was founded in 1877. In 1911, 1617 stallions were exported from Great Britain.

- **Although no longer** required to work on farms, the breed is now popular for showing and breeding.

▶ *These shires horses are shown in harness as a working pair. This breed should have a slightly Roman or convex nose, and large, wide set eyes.*

Welsh Ponies and Cobs

- **The Welsh breed** is split into four sections: A, B, C, and D.

- **The original** and smallest of the Welsh breeds is the Welsh Mountain Pony (Section A). It stands no more than 12 hh and is most commonly gray – although it can be any color except piebald and skewbald. The head should be small with neat pointed ears, big bold eyes, and a wide forehead.

▲ *The Welsh Cob makes an excellent driving pony*

- **Section B** is the Welsh Pony. These ponies were used by farmers to herd sheep and other ponies. Today the breed is mainly used as riding ponies for children. They are shown and ridden in jumping competitions.

- **Section C** is the Welsh Pony of Cob type. This pony is stronger than the Welsh Pony and was originally used for farm work. A versatile breed, they are ideal for both for riding and driving.

- **Section D** is the Welsh Cob and the tallest of the breed. These cobs are noted for courage and endurance and are strong and agile.

- **The Welsh Ponies** and Cobs (Section B, C, and D) have the same coloring as the Welsh Mountain Pony (Section A).

- **The Welsh Section B and C** do not exceed 13.2 hh. Welsh Section D cobs exceed 13.2 hh.

- **Welsh Ponies** and Cobs are renowned for being sure-footed, hardy, and natural jumpers.

- **The Welsh Pony and Cob Society** was established in 1901 and published the first volume of the Welsh Stud Book in 1902.

...FASCINATING FACT...
Welsh Ponies have been bred in the Welsh
mountains since before Roman times.

Highland and Shetland

- **The Shetland** and Highland pony breeds both originate from the far north of the British Isles.

- **Native to** the Shetland Islands off northern Scotland, the Shetland is the smallest British native pony. The breed standard states that they should not be any taller than 42 in (107 cm) high. They are generally measured in inches or centimeters rather than hands. Shetlands were originally used as working ponies carrying peat and seaweed.

  - **There are miniature** Shetland Ponies that should not exceed 34 in (87 cm) high.

    - **Shetland Ponies** can be of any color except spotted. The breed has a double coat with guard hairs in winter to help keep out the wind and rain. They also have particularly thick manes and tails to help keep them warm. In summer, they develop a short, shiny coat.

    - **The Shetland** is an extremely strong pony, and is thought to be the strongest of all breeds for its size.

    - **There have been Shetland Ponies** on the Shetland Islands for over 2,000 years. Over the past 200 years, they have been exported all over the world.

◄ *Shetland ponies were used as pit ponies in the mining industry, but are now popular for driving, showing and as children's ponies.*

- **The Highland** is the largest of the Scottish breeds, standing between 12 hh and 14 hh.

- **The breed originated** in the Highlands of Scotland. There are two types: the Mainland, which is larger, and the smaller Island Pony.

- **Highland ponies** come in a variety of colors including dun, brown, bay, and black and Highland Ponies bred on the island of Rhum show unusual colors, such as chestnut with a silver mane.

- **Crofters used Highland Ponies** for haulage and farm work, and they are still used on many hunting estates to transport deer and game. Highland Ponies are also used for trekking, riding for the disabled, and as all-round family ponies.

▲ *The Highland is an ancient breed that can survive on scarce grazing.*

Dartmoor and Exmoor

▲ *The Dartmoor Pony is the symbol of the Dartmoor National Park.*

- **The Dartmoor** is a small pony no bigger than 12.2 hh and is usually colored black, bay, or brown.

- **The ancient breed** is native to Dartmoor in Devon, England.

- **Dartmoor** is an exposed area of moorland standing over 300 m (1,000 ft) above sea level. This has resulted in the breed evolving into a hardy, sure-footed pony which can survive on limited grazing.

- **Dartmoor Ponies** are particularly noted for their calm temperament and lack of excitability, making them suitable for children to ride and look after. They are also ideal for driving and showing.

> **...FASCINATING FACT...**
> Until the 1960s, Dartmoor Ponies were used to escort
> inmates from the local prison while on outside duties.

- **As well as being used** on farms Dartmoor Ponies have been used to transport tin from the mines.

- **The Exmoor Pony** has inhabited the Exmoor moorland of southwest Britain for many years. They are brown, bay, or dun colored with lighter markings around their eyes and muzzles. They stand at about 12 hh.

- **Exmoor ponies** are thought to have existed since prehistoric times, but are now a very rare breed. Today there is thought to be fewer than 200 ponies living on Exmoor.

- **In the past**, farmers used Exmoor Ponies for agricultural work and shepherding. They are very strong, and able to carry adult riders easily.

- **Because of its strength** the Exmoor is not ideally suited for children who are beginning to ride, but with a competent rider they can take part in showing, jumping, and long-distance riding.

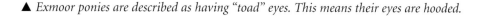

▲ *Exmoor ponies are described as having "toad" eyes. This means their eyes are hooded.*

111

Connemara and New Forest

- **The Connemara** is the only native pony of Ireland. They are usually gray, black, brown, or dun and occasionally roan, chestnut, or palomino, measuring between 13 hh and 14.2 hh.

- **Connemara Ponies** were mostly used by farmers to transport heavy goods, such as peat, potatoes, and seaweed and pull a trap for family transportation. Today, they are used as children's ponies, and for competing, driving, and showing.

- **Connemaras are intelligent** and willing, as well as agile and obedient.

- **Hardy**, athletic, and with good balance, the Connemara is also strong and free-moving.

◄ *The Connemara makes an excellent competition pony for teenagers or small adults.*

- **The Connemara breed** is often crossed with the Thoroughbred or Arab. These part-bred horses make successful competition horses in dressage, showjumping, and three-day eventing.

- **The New Forest Pony** comes from southern England, where it can still be found living wild in the New Forest region. They are usually bay, brown, or gray, standing 12 hh to 14.2 hh and make excellent riding ponies.

- **The New Forest** Breeding and Cattle Society produced its first stud book in 1960. The breed rules permit any color except piebald, skewbald, or blue-eyed cream.

- **New Forest Ponies** are naturally sure-footed and hardy.

- **A long smooth stride** makes New Forest Ponies comfortable to ride and they are ideal for trekking and endurance.

▶ *A quality New Forest Pony excels in the show ring.*

113

Fell and Dales

▶ *The Dales Pony combines good conformation with energy and ability, making the breed ideal for riding and driving.*

- **Fell and Dales** pony breeds originated in the north of England. The two breeds are genetically related, with the Fell being slightly smaller and lighter in build than the Dales.

- **Dales Ponies** on average stand between 13.2 hh and 14.2 hh. They are mostly black, but there are also bays and a few grays.

- **In the 19th century**, Dales Ponies were used for agricultural work and to carry lead from mines to the ports. They are known as good trotters with considerable stamina and a docile temperament.

- **Dales Ponies** are often used as trekking ponies as they are capable of carrying adults. They are also popular for general-riding, showing, and driving.

- **The Dales Pony** almost became extinct in the 1950s, but numbers increased after the formation of the Dales Pony Society in 1963.

- **Fell Ponies** were traditionally used as pack ponies carrying lead from the mines. They were also used for pulling carts and trotting races.

- **Fell Ponies** vary in height between 13 hh and 14 hh.

- **The breed standards** of the Fell Pony allow black, brown, bay, or gray, preferably with no white markings. They have long manes and tails, and silky feathering on their legs.

- **Fell Ponies** are an old breed, dating back to Roman times when they were used as draft animals.

- **Fell Ponies** are renowned for their good paces. Their active walk and fast trot makes them an ideal driving pony.

▼ *The constitution of the Fell Pony is said to be "as hard as iron."*

Akhal-Teke

- **The Akhal-Teke** is an ancient breed that dates back over 3,000 years.

- **The breed originated** from the Turkoman Steppes in Central Asia and takes its name from a nomadic tribe known as Teke found at the Akhal oasis.

- **The average height** is between 14.2 hh and 15.2 hh and an Akhal-Teke may be dun, bay, chestnut, gray, or black with a short and silky tail. The head of an Akhal-Teke is similar to an Arab's and its body is described as one of the most elegant in the horse world.

- **The breed** is noted for stamina and endurance. This was shown in 1935 when a group of Akhal-Teke horses were taken on a three-day trek across the desert to Moscow without water.

- **Developed to suit** desert conditions, the Akhal-Teke horse has fine skin with a long back and narrow quarters.

- **Today,** they are used in many different disciplines including racing and endurance.

- **In history** Akhal-Teke have been prized by Alexander the Great, Genghis Khan, and Marco Polo. Alexander the Great even erected a tomb to commemorate his Akhal-Teke stallion, Bucephalus.

- **The Turkmenistan's** national emblem features the breed.

- **The rider of an Akhal-Teke** needs to be confident and calm as they are known to have sensitive natures and to dislike strangers.

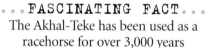

...FASCINATING FACT...
The Akhal-Teke has been used as a racehorse for over 3,000 years

▼ *This herd of Akhal-Teke horses show the wide range of colors common to their breed.*

Haflinger and Icelandic

- **A pony standing** between 13.1 hh and 14.2 hh, the Haflinger is palomino or chestnut with a light-colored mane and tail. The breed takes its name from the village of Haflinger near the border of Austria and Italy.

- **The Haflinger** is a small, strong pony. It has a slightly dished face and large eyes, and enjoys exercise.

- **Haflingers** make good riding ponies, but are very versatile and can be used for driving, endurance, and even as vaulting ponies for acrobatic displays. They have also proved a popular breed with centers for disabled riders because of their honest, calm natures.

- **Haflingers** are now established around the world and a register of pure-bred Haflinger stallions has been kept for over 100 years.

- **As there is no word** for pony in Icelandic, the Icelandic, although under 13.2 hh, is always referred to as a horse.

- **Icelandic horses** have three layers to their coats to help them withstand the harsh climate in which they live.

- **The Icelandic breed** is long-lived, and an animal is not considered mature until seven years old.

- **Icelandic horses** can be of any color, have a stocky build and are noted for good eyesight and tough nature.

- **The horses still play** a large part in Icelandic life. As well as being excellent family riding horses, they compete in showing, endurance, and special race meetings.

...**FASCINATING FACT**...
In Italy in 2003 the first cloned horse
was born to a Haflinger mare.

▼ *Haflingers are small and
strong. They are a hardy breed
ideally suited to working on
mountain slopes.*

121

Appaloosa and Dutch Warmblood

- **The Appaloosa** is an ancient breed depicted in prehistoric cave paintings. It is known for its spotted coat that comes in a variety of recognized patterns, but the breed can also have whole color coats. The main patterns are known as blanket, spots, leopard, snowflake, and frost. They often have black-and-white markings on their feet.

- **The base color** of an Appaloosa's coat can be a variety of different colors, including bay, black, chestnut, and palomino. They have short manes and tails and usually stand between 14.2 hh and 16 hh.

▼ *Over 500,000 Appaloosas are registered in the Appaloosa Horse Club today. The club was established in 1938.*

- **In the US**, Appaloosas were developed by the Nez Perce—Native American Indians who lived in north-west America. The breed was virtually destroyed in the late 1800s when the US army captured the Nez Perce Indians and killed their horses.

- **The word Appaloosa** is derived from Palouse country, an area surrounding the Palouse River. Today, Appaloosas are prized for endurance riding, because of their strength and strong limbs.

- **The Dutch Warmblood** originated in Holland and usually stands between 15.2 hh and 17 hh.

- **Dutch Warmbloods** are usually chestnut, bay, black, or gray with white markings on the face and legs.

- **There are two distinct types** of Dutch Warmbloods: the heavier horse, called a Groningen, which is used in agriculture, and the lighter Gelderland, which is a driving and riding horse that also excels in showjumping.

- **Initially used** by farmers for agricultural work, Dutch Warmbloods have been subjected to strict breeding programs to encourage the best conformation possible.

- **The Gelderlander** is recognized as a brilliant sports performance horse.

> **...FASCINATING FACT...**
> All Appaloosa foals are born with light coats
> that eventually grow darker. However, grays start
> dark and become lighter.

Andalucian and Lipizzaner

- **The Andalucian** stands between 15 hh and 16.2 hh. The breed originates from Spain and was the chosen warhorse of the Spanish conquistadors.

- **Andalucian coats** are usually gray or black, but can also be dun and palomino. One of their coat colors is called mulberry—a dappled gray with hints of purple. The breed has strong rear quarters with thick manes and tails.

- **The Andalucian breed** is noted for its intelligence, beauty, and sensitivity and they can make excellent dressage horses.

- **In medieval times**, Andalucian horses were bred and protected by Carthusian monks.

- **In Spain**, Andalucians are called *pura espagnol* or "pure Spanish horses."

- **Lipizzaners are used** at The Spanish Riding School of Vienna— the oldest riding school in the world. These horses are taught special movements, involving controlled athletic jumps and kicks known as "airs above ground." The movements are said to be based on medieval tricks of war that were used to evade enemy soldiers.

- **Lipizzaners** usually have gray coats. The foals are born black or brown and develop their gray coats as they mature. This can take as long as ten years.

- **The ancestry** of the Lipizzaner dates back to AD800. They are a result of crossing Berber horses from North Africa with horses used by the Romans for chariot racing known as Karst horses.

- **Archduke Charles II of Austria** founded a special stud at Lipizza (Lipica) in 1580 to produce the best horses possible from where the Lipizzaner breed takes its name.

- **One of the most famous** movements performed by the Lipizzaner during displays is the *ballotade*. The horse leaps into the air while keeping its legs tucked underneath it.

▶ *A Lipizzaner demonstrating the* levade *where it takes its weight on the hind quarters in a controlled manner while raising the upper body and tucking in its front legs.*

Tennessee Walking Horse and Morgan

- **Roy Rogers**, the famous television cowboy, rode a Tennessee Walking Horse called Trigger. This breed has a particular gait that resembles a running walk.

- **Tennessee Walking Horses** range in size from 15 hh to 17 hh and come in a variety of colors, including black, bay, or chestnut.

▶ *Morgans are popular ridden showhorses.*

- **With long tails** that are high set and a deep muscular chest, Tennessee Walking Horses are said to be particularly calm and good-natured horses.

- **The first horse** to develop the gliding walk was born in 1837. This trait was developed by farmers and plantation owners in Tennessee who wanted a horse capable of covering long distances with a smooth stride. Some Tennessee Walking Horses are said to click their teeth in time to the rhythm of the walk.

- **The Tennessee Walking Horse** has become so popular that it is one of the top ten breeds recognized in the US.

- **The Morgan** originates from Vermont and dates back to the 18th century. The breed can be traced back to one stallion who took its name from its owner, Justin Morgan.

- **On average** Morgans stand between 14.1 hh and 15.2 hh. They are primarily brown, bay, black, or chestnut.

- **The eyes** should be large and prominent and its shapely ears set wide apart. Mares often have longer ears than stallions.

- **The breed** is noted for strength and particularly gentle temperament.

- **The Morgan Horse Club** was founded in 1909 to stop the decline in the breed. Today, they compete in many disciplines including showing, dressage, jumping, and driving.

Cleveland Bay and Hanoverian

- **The Cleveland Bay** is the oldest breed of English horse.
- **Cleveland Bays** stand between 15.3 hh and 17 hh, and as the name suggests are bay colored, without feathering on the legs. They take their name from the area of North England where they were originally bred.
- **In the mid-eighteenth century**, Cleveland Bays were known as Chapman horses. Chapmen were early traveling salesmen who used the horses to transport their goods. They were also used in agriculture. They are known to live a long time and mature at about six years old.

◀ *Cleveland Bays make excellent driving horses because of their good temperament and endurance.*

- **Cleveland Bays** are intelligent with good temperament and were popular carriage horses. They were used by the British cavalry in the World War I and even today British royalty use them to pull state coaches.

- **The Cleveland Bay** is often crossed with the Thoroughbred, the resulting part-bred animal makes an excellent competition horse.

▲ *The identifying "H" brand mark of a pure Hanoverian.*

- **The Hanoverian** originates from Germany. A tall horse, the breed stands between 16 hh and 17 hh and may come in any solid color.

- **The excellent gaits** of the Hanoverian include a ground covering walk, a free-moving trot, and a rhythmic canter.

- **Originally**, Hanoverians were bred for the military and as strong carriage horses. They are noted for their strong backs.

- **Hanoverians are now bred** as performance horses and are winners at Olympic level in showjumping and dressage. They also excel in driving and eventing.

> ...**FASCINATING FACT**...
> It is believed Cleveland Bays evolved from
> the horses left in Britain by the Romans.

Mustang, Paint, and Pinto

- **The word Mustang** is derived from a Spanish word meaning "stray" or "ownerless."

- **Mustang horses** were introduced to the US around the 1700s by Spanish settlers, but animals were abandoned and broke free to form huge herds that numbered about two million by 1900.

  - **In order to protect** grassland grazing for cattle, the Mustangs were culled and by 1970 their numbers were reduced to less than 17,000. They are now a protected breed and their numbers are managed.

◀ *The Pinto horse was first introduced into North America by Spanish explorers.*

- **Mustangs** stand between 13 hh and 16 hh and can be of any color.

- **Mustangs were used** by both the Native American Indians and cowboys.

- **American Paint Horses** are clearly defined by both coat patterning and conformation. They have to come from stock recognized by the American Paint Horse Association, the American Quarter Horse Association, or the Jockey Club. Their coats are a mixture of white and any other color.

- **There are three** recognized coat patterns for Paint Horses called Tobiano, Overo, and Tovero. The patterns relate to how the pattern of markings covers the horse's body and legs. For example, the Tobiano generally has white legs and the Overo usually has one or more dark colored legs.

- **The Paint Horse** is valued as being a strong versatile horse that excels both as a leisure riding horse and in competition.

- **The Pinto horse** was associated with the North American Indians and was believed to have special magical powers in battle.

- **The Pinto Horse Association of America** recognizes different breeds and cross-breeds as long as they have the required coloring.

Other pony breeds

- **Przewalski's Horse** takes its name from a Russian explorer, Colonel Nikolai Przewalski, who is said to have discovered the breed in Mongolia in 1881. A small stubborn breed, it stands between 12 hh and 14 hh and is dun colored with a dorsal stripe along the back and zebra stripes on the legs. It has an erect mane and dark brown tail.

- **Camargue Ponies** originate from Southern France. Many still live in wild herds on salt marshes in the Camargue region.

- **The rare Eriskay Pony** is an ancient breed found on the island of Eriskay in the Hebrides, off Scotland. These hardy ponies were originally used by crofters to carry peat and seaweed.

- **Chinoteagues** are the only pony native to the US. They stand about 12 hh and are extremely hardy, able to survive on little vegetation. A number of wild ponies still live on the islands off the Virginian coast.

◀ *The extravagant action of the Hackney makes him unsuitable as a riding pony, but excellent as a driving pony.*

▶ *Fjord Ponies traditionally have their coarse manes trimmed in a crescent shape with the dark central hair left slightly longer.*

- **The Fjord Pony** was used in battle by the Vikings and also for plowing. They are striking-looking ponies, standing between 14 hh and 14.2 hh, dun colored with a dorsal stripe.

- **The Hackney** is a showy, high-stepping horse or pony. The pony stands under 14 hh – the horse 14 hh to 16 hh.

- **The Newfoundland Pony** developed from a cross of British native ponies. Standing 11 hh to 14.2 hh, they are usually brown with a thick mane and tail. Over recent decades, their numbers have dipped and efforts are being made to increase the population.

- **The Caspian** is one of the oldest equine breeds. These small ponies stand up to 12 hh and are bold and fast-moving, making them ideal for competitive scurry driving.

- **The Konik Pony** is widespread throughout Poland and in rural areas is still used in agricultural work.

> ....FASCINATING FACT....
> Camargue Ponies are usually gray and are
> known as the "white horse of the sea."

Other horse breeds

- **The American Standardbred** is the most popular harness racer in the world. The name "Standardbred" was used because horses had to reach a certain standard over a mile to be registered as part of the new breed.

- **The Brabant**, or Belgium Heavy Draft, is descended from the medieval heavy war horse. It is the most popular draft breed in the US. These large horses stand between 16 hh and 18 hh and are usually chestnut or roan with light manes and tails.

- **The Trakehner** stands between 16 hh and 16.2 hh and can be any color. The breed originates from Prussia where a stud was established in 1732.

- **The Percheron** is a strong, heavyweight horse, standing 15 hh to 17 hh. Usually gray or black in color, this breed originated in France and has developed into one of the strongest draft horses in the world.

- **The Yili** from China is a new breed, developed from crossing Russian horses with native stock. They are described as draft/riding horses standing about 14 hh and usually bay in color. They can cover long distances at speed because of their excellent stamina.

▲ *Percherons have broad chests with strong forearms and excellent feet.*

- **The Canadian Horse** is renowned for its stamina, versatility, and willingness to please. Because of their hardiness, they became known as the "little iron horse." They are usually black, standing 14 hh to 16 hh and have docile characters.

- **American Saddlebred** horses usually stands at around 16 hh. They are popular riding and driving horses.

- **The Falabella** is the best-known miniature horse breed. They are usually about 30 in (76 cm) tall at the withers.

- **Mostly chestnut** and standing over 16 hh, the versatile Selle Français is successful as an all-round competition horse. Its name means "French saddle horse."

- **The Holsteiner** is one of Germany's oldest warmblood breeds and is successful in all spheres of competition.

▶ *The American Saddlebred is a specialist breed that has a high-stepping action and is a popular show horse.*

Western riding

- **Western riding** is not confined to the U.S.A. It is popular worldwide.

- **This form of riding** was developed by the cowboys in the United States and was brought to the Americas by the Spanish.

- **Unlike English-style riders**, western riders do not always wear protective headgear. The traditional clothing is a Stetson hat, shirt, riding chaps (worn over pants), and gloves. Riders may also wear three-quarter length decorated leather cowboy boots.

- **Western riders** use their weight and neck reining to influence their horse's speed and direction.

▶ *This horse is wearing a typical Western bridle and saddle kept in place with a breastplate. The rider wears a Stetson, chaps, and cowboy boots.*

▶ *More than any other item of clothing, the Stetson typifies the western cowboy. It gives protection against the weather.*

- **By holding the reins** in one hand western-style riders have one hand free. This enabled cowboys to hold a rope when catching livestock.

- **Reining** has developed to competition level. Riders carry out a set of movements, including slides, turns, and circles. They are judged on their accuracy and the obedience of their horse.

- **On dismounting,** the western-style rider removes his right leg from the stirrup, swings his leg over the saddle, and then steps down with his left leg. In English-style riding, both legs are removed from the stirrups prior to dismounting.

- **In western riding,** the canter is called a lope and the trot is known as a jog.

- **The rodeo** developed out of ranch riding and includes skills, such as saddle-bronco riding, bareback-bronco riding, and bull riding. There are also timed events involving roping, barrel racing, and steer wrestling.

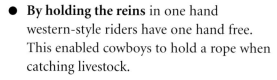

...FASCINATING FACT...
The Stetson was named after John Batterson Stetson, the inventor of the cowboy hat.

Horse racing

- **Horse racing** is a worldwide sport. One of the most popular forms of the race is over flat ground when Thoroughbreds are raced over distances, varying from three-quarters of a mile to two miles.

- **Horse racing** became a popular sport during the 18th and 19th centuries when many of Britain's famous horse races were created, such as the Derby in 1780 and the Grand National in 1839.

- **Steeplechases** were originally run from one church steeple to another. Any fences or walls in between the two points had to be jumped.

- **The Kentucky Derby** is the most famous horse race in the U.S.A. and has been held since 1875.

- **Horse racing** was illegal in England between 1649 and 1658 when the country was controlled by Oliver Cromwell.

▼ *The Curragh is the headquarters of flat racing in Ireland and can trace its history back to the third century and chariot racing.*

...FASCINATING FACT...
The Dubai World Cup is the world's richest
horse race with a prize fund of $6 million.

- **Saddles** designed for flat racing can weigh as little as 8 oz (0.2 kg).

- **Point-to-point** is a race over jumps for amateur jockeys. Their mount has to have hunted at least seven times in the past season.

- **Before motorized transportation**, racehorses had to walk to race meetings. They often had to set off weeks before the race was due to begin, in order to give them time to recover.

- **Jockeys** race in "silks." These are colors—a colored hat cover and jacket —that identify the horse's owner.

▶ *Racehorses are trained to go into starting stalls which help prevent false starts.*

Horse shows

◀ *Inhand showing classes involve the horse being led around the ring by a handler. The horse is shown without a saddle.*

- **Horse shows** are held all over the world and offer the opportunity for horseowners to compete against other similar horses and ponies. Classes are held for specific breeds and types and for all levels of rider.

- **Before the show**, the horse is groomed and the tack cleaned.

- **The show and classes** chosen should be appropriate for the level of the horse and rider.

- **Entries and fees** should be sent in advance if necessary and transportation arranged.

- **The day before** the show, every effort should be made to ensure the horse looks its best. A thorough grooming session should take place, leaving the mane and tail plaiting until the morning of the show.

- **Equipment** needed for a show includes: feed and water, a grooming kit, a first-aid kit, tack, and the rider's clothing.

- **The morning of a show**, the horse should be fed, groomed, and any plaits required put in the mane and tail. It will also need to be dressed appropriately for traveling.

- **Enough time** should be allowed for a calm loading and relaxed drive to the event.

- **The rider** should check the show schedules to make sure there has not been a change to the running order and report to the show secretary to collect their number.

- **The horse** should be lightly exercised prior to going into the show ring to work off excess energy.

◄ *On arrival at the showground, the horse should be unloaded and allowed to stretch its legs and become accustomed to the surroundings.*

Mounted games

- **Mounted games** or gymkhanas should be good fun for all who take part —from parents leading children on ponies, to competitive teenagers.

- **Games** are varied and often include sack, flag, walk-and-trot, egg-and-spoon, and bending poles.

▼ *The pony and rider need to be balanced and supple. In the flag race, the rider has to lean over to grab the flag whilst moving and turning at speed.*

- **Games are usually** divided up into leading rein races for small children and rider age groups.

- **Rosettes** are awarded for first, second, and third places in each event and points are given—the overall champion being awarded a trophy.

- **A good games pony** is calm, but fast-moving and able to stop suddenly. The good gymkhana rider is well-balanced, stable, and able to get on and off a pony easily.

- **Riders** should make sure their pony is not afraid of flapping flags or other race equipment and is happy to run alongside them during race activities.

- **In the U.S.A**, the Pony Club runs mounted games competitions with regional and championship finals.

- **No whips** or spurs are allowed in the games. The rider should wear a safety hat, jodhpurs, and riding boots with an optional body protector.

- **The pony** should wear a snaffle bit. Martingales are also allowed.

- **The word gymkhana** comes from India, where mounted games have been played for hundreds of years.

Dressage and showing

- **Dressage** allows a horse and rider to show themselves to be working in harmony.

- **Tests** from novice to advanced levels are carried out in arenas. The horse and rider are judged on how well they execute their movements.

- **Faults** during a dressage test include ignoring the rider's aids, being in the wrong gait, and loosing impulsion and rhythm.

▲ *An advanced dressage rider, wearing top hat and tails, works at showing the fluidity of the horse's movements.*

- **Showing classes** are categorized in many different ways. For example, inhand classes where the horse is led around the ring in front of a judge and ridden classes.

- **The judge** pays attention to how the horse moves, its behavior, suitability, appearance, and conformation.

- **The different classes** of showing include: individual breeds, halter, equitation, hunter, saddle-horse, and parade.

▼ *Native ponies do not have their manes or tails plaited or trimmed for the show ring and are shown in their natural state.*

- **In some ridden show classes**, a judge will ride a horse, as well as watch the animal perform with its rider.

- **In ridden show classes**, riders are required to exhibit horses individually as well as in a group. During this time the judge assesses the behavior, conformation, and paces of the horses.

- **A good showhorse** must be obedient and show no sign of disobeying its rider or displaying any aggression toward other animals.

- **Turn out** is all important in showing and great attention is paid to the detail of mane-plaiting to show off a good head and neck.

▶ *A special inhand bridle is often used for showing classes. The leather can be lighter or more finely tooled than general-purpose tack to show off a horse's best features.*

143

Showjumping

- **Showjumping** competitions are usually restricted to competitors of a certain age, their animal's height, or its level of experience.

- **As well as individual** jumping competitions, there are pairs and team events and sometimes even costume jumping.

- **The competitors** are allowed to walk the course before the competition begins in order to memorize it and work out any tricky stride patterns.

▼ *Showjumping takes the form of a course of colored jumps set out in an arena.*

- **A "fault"** is a penalty incurred if a competitor knocks down or refuses a jump, or exceeds the time allowed. If the horse refuses a fence a second time, they are eliminated from the competition.

- **All the riders** who manage a clear round without any faults qualify for a second round of jumping. This is usually a timed, shorter course over higher jumps. The winner has the fewest faults and best time.

- **Jumps** may be uprights or spreads. Uprights are straight up-and-down jumps. Spreads are broad jumps with two sets of uprights. All the fences fall if knocked by a horse.

- **A course is set out** to include turns and combination fences, such as double and triples. These are set closer together than other jumps and care must be taken to approach them at the correct angle and speed.

- **Water jumps** may also be included – either broad troughs of water with a low fence at the front, or a ditch and higher fence. If the horse puts a foot in the water they are awarded a fault.

- **A good showjumping horse** is courageous, quick, agile, and athletic, but willing to listen to the rider.

> ... **FASCINATING FACT** ...
> Top Puissance horses can jump over
> 7 ft (2.13 m) in height.

Cross-country and eventing

▲ *This horse and rider confidently jump a cross-country fence in water.*

- **A cross-country** course is demanding in requiring high levels of fitness and stamina. There are different levels of cross-country, from beginner through to advanced. Cross-country jumps are immovable and require great courage from both horse and rider.

- **A horse and rider** have to complete the cross-country course within a set time. Penalties are given for falls and refusals, as well as time faults.

- **Event horses** have to be at least five years old to compete.

- **Competitors** are be disqualified if they take the wrong course, fall off twice, or refuse a jump three times.

146

- **The jumps** are spread out and riders have to pay attention to the condition of the ground to get the best of their horses.

- **As well as individual competitions**, there are team and pairs events.

- **The rider** has a chance to walk the course before competing to study the jumps, and the various options they might give. There are sometimes easier but slower ways to approach certain jumps.

- **In horse trials**, the events or "phases" are spread over one, two or three days. Competitors take part in dressage, showjumping, and cross-country, with extra road and track, and steeplechase sections. The horse with the fewest penalty points wins.

- **The dressage test** aims to show that a courageous horse capable of showjumping and cross-country tests is also disciplined and obedient.

- **The road and track** sections do not involve jumps, but test stamina at trot and canter and the steeplechase section involves jumping brush fences.

▶ *Jumping into and out of water requires a bold and confident horse. A high level of trust and communication between horse and rider is important to be successful in cross-country events.*

Driving

- **Driving** was internationally recognized as a competitive sport in 1969.
- **Driving trials** follow a similar format to ridden three-day events. The competition consists of three phases, A, B, and C and uses a penalty-scoring system.

▼ *A pair of driving horses negotiating a water hazard. The driver needs to be precise in giving instructions and the horses obedient and responsive. Driving trials usually have divisions for singles, pairs, tandems, and teams of four.*

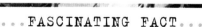
▶ *Driving bridles incorporate blinkers. This prevents the horse from becoming frightened at the sight of the moving wheels behind it.*

- **Phase A** takes place in a large arena and the competitors have to drive a sequence of set movements. Marks are awarded for obedience, quality of paces, and style.

- **Phase B** is a marathon over varying distances. The timed sections have to be completed at different paces.

- **Phase C** is an obstacle test around a course of cones. This phase tests the driver's skill and the obedience of the driving horses.

- **Scurry driving** involves driving a pair of ponies around a mini-obstacle course against the clock.

- **Scurry competitions** are normally divided into two sections: 12 hh (48 in) and under, and 12 hh to 14.2 hh (48 in to 58 in).

- **Show-ring driving** is judged on the quality of the turnout—horse, vehicle, harness, and driver—and style and performance.

- **Large horse** shows often have classes for heavy harness horses.

> ...**FASCINATING FACT**...
> HRH The Duke of Edinburgh competed a
> team of Fell Ponies in driving trials.

149

Endurance riding

- **The Tevis Cup**, or the Western States Trail Ride is a one-day, 100-mi (160-km) ride in California and is the oldest modern-day endurance ride. It first began in 1955 and has been run annually ever since.

- **The welfare** of the horse is of utmost importance and competitors can be disqualified on the ruling of a vet.

- **The motto** of the sport of endurance is "to complete is to win."

- **There are different kinds** of endurance ride: races when all the competitors start at the same time and non-competitive pleasure or training rides. There are also set speed, graded, and endurance rides. Rides vary in length from up to 20 mi (30 km) to over 100 mi (160 km).

◀ The sport of endurance requires a strong partnership between horse and rider. The intensive level of fitness training helps build this bond.

- **At the lower levels** of the sport, any horse who is fit can enter. Although Arabs tend to excel at long-distance riding, cobs and ponies are just as likely to take part on 20 mi (30 km) rides.

- **Before taking part** in a ride, the horse will have its feet and shoes checked by a farrier, be trotted up before a vet to satisfy them that the horse is sound, and have his heart rate taken. The vet will also check the animal for any bumps, abrasions, or cuts.

- **Along the ride** are checkpoints where riders identify themselves to officials, and crew stops where back-up crew can refresh the horse and offer both the horse and rider a drink. Vet checks are made in longer rides.

- **On finishing a competitive ride**, the rider has to report back to the vet within a set time to re-present his horse for examination. Ribbons are awarded for completion of the ride and on the condition of the horse.

- **There are restrictions** on the age a horse can take part in endurance rides. A horse cannot be younger than seven years old to take part in more advanced rides.

> **...FASCINATING FACT...**
> The most well-known long-distance ride in
> Great Britain is the Golden Horseshoe—a two-
> day endurance ride over 100 mi (160 km).

Western and rodeo

- **The first rodeo** is believed to have been held in Arizona in 1866.

- **The first regulation** and organization of rodeos began in the 1930s with the formation of the Rodeo Association of America (RAA) and the Cowboys Turtle Association (CTA).

- **There are five basic events** in a rodeo: calf roping, steer wrestling, saddle-bronco, bareback, and bull riding. There are large money prizes for event winners, but it is an extremely dangerous sport and injuries are common.

- **In the bucking competitions**, the rider must stay on the animal for ten seconds for saddle-bronco riding and eight seconds for bareback-bronco riding.

- **In calf roping**, riders have to lasso a calf from their horse, tie their rope to the saddle, dismount and tie the calf's legs together.

▲ *This western display team shows the precision and skill of the western horse and rider.*

◄ *Barrel racing competitions are timed and contestants are penalized for knocking over a barrel.*

- **Steer** (a young castrated bull) wrestling involves the rider called a bull dogger leaping from his horse to take hold of the steer's head and wrestling him to the ground. A second cowboy called a hazer stops the steer veering away from the rider before it is caught.

- **Special cutting horses** are used to separate out steers from a herd. They are skilled at isolating the chosen animal without splitting up the rest of the group.

- **Barrel racing** is an exciting timed competition in which horses race around three barrels in a cloverleaf pattern.

- **Reining competitions** are ridden at speed. The horse and rider show co-operation and agility while demonstrating particular movements.

- **The horse** is expected to show quick stops, turns and pivots—where a horse turns 90 degrees from a halt by pivoting on its hindquarters.

Polo

- **Polo** was introduced to the west by British cavalry officers serving in India in the 19th century.

- **A fast team game**, polo is now played worldwide.

- **There are a number** of different forms, but standard polo involves two teams of four riders, aiming to score goals by hitting a ball through goalposts with a polo stick from horseback. The polo stick is called a mallet.

▶ *Polo riders wear special helmets, protective knee pads, and boots. Their ponies wear leg and tail protection.*

- **The polo ball** is a difficult target to hit, being only 3 in (8 cm) in diameter. It is usually made of willow root or plastic.

- **The game** is split into timed sections called chukkas which allow the ponies to rest between play.

- **A trained polo pony** is worth a great deal of money. It is fast, agile, and able to stop instantly from a gallop, and take off again at speed.

- **Polo ponies** are taught to turn at speed and to lean into other ponies.

- **Each rider** is allowed to ride more than one pony in the course of a polo game.

- **Argentina** is a country noted for breeding quality polo ponies.

▶ *Polo ponies have hogged or shaved manes and are usually small Thoroughbreds.*

....**FASCINATING FACT**...
The word polo originates from the Tibetan word *pulu* meaning ball.

Harness racing

- **Harness racing** is one of the most popular equestrian sports in the world.

- **There are two different gaits** or types of harness-racing horse: the pace horse and the trotting horse.

- **The pace horse**, or pacer, moves its legs in lateral pairs and usually wears special leg hobbles when racing to maintain the pace.

- **The trotting horse**, or trotter, moves its legs in diagonal pairs.

- **If a horse breaks out** of the trot pace, the driver must pull over to the outside of the racetrack, thus losing ground on the other racers.

▼ *Harness-racing drivers wear safety helmets and goggles to protect themselves. They are permitted to carry a whip.*

- **The horse pulls** a sulky—a lightweight two-wheeled vehicle.

- **A mobile starting gate** is used in harness racing to ensure a fair start for all competitors.

- **Harness racing** is held on a snow track at St Moritz in Switzerland. A special sulky sleigh is used to suit the conditions.

- **Horses often wear** thick sheepskin nosebands called shadow rolls. These limit the horses' view of the ground and prevents them from shying at shadows.

▶ *Pacers usually wear hobbles to prevent them from breaking their gait.*

157

Olympic Games

- **Three-day eventing** and dressage were introduced to the Olympics in 1912. Today there are individual and team events in the three disciplines.

- **The first Olympic team** dressage competition was won by Germany in 1928.

- **Riding events** are the only competitions at Olympic level where men and women compete equally. However, this was not always the case. When the modern Olympics began, only male riders who were officers in the cavalry could take part in the three-day event.

- **In 1900,** there were competitions to judge the best equestrian long jump and high jump but these were dropped from the Olympics shortly afterward.

▲ *Gold medal winning countries in the equestrian events at the Olympic games in Sydney in 2000 were the U.S.A., Germany, the Netherlands, and Australia.*

◄ *Introduced in 1900, showjumping was the first equestrian sport in the modern Olympic games. At least one of the colors of the Olympic rings is represented in the flag of every participating nation.*

- **Women** were only allowed to compete in Olympic dressage for the first time in 1952.

- **Liselott Linsenhoff** was the first woman to win gold in an equestrian event as part of the German dressage team, in 1968. In 1972, she was the first woman to win Olympic gold in the individual dressage.

- **Bill Roycroft** of Australia left hospital with a broken collar bone to compete for his country in 1960 in the three-day team event. They went on to win gold.

- **Another hero** of the games was Lis Hartel of Denmark who won a silver medal in dressage despite having to be helped on and off her horse. She had been paralyzed by polio in 1944.

- **In 1968**, British rider Jane Bullen was the first woman to win gold in the three-day event.

> ...FASCINATING FACT...
> In 680BC, chariot racing was the first
> horse sport at the Olympic Games.

▶ *Dutch rider, Joroen Dubbeldam, and Sjiem
celebrate winning the showjumping individual
gold medal at the 2000 Sydney Olympics .*

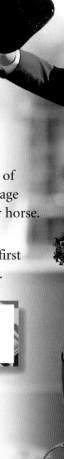

Other horse sports

- **Drag hunting** does not involve killing an animal, but riders follow a artificial scent laid by a human runner.

- **The drag hunt** uses hounds to track the scent, which is laid over open country. The huntsmen and hunt follow, jumping obstacles in their course.

- **Vaulting** is gymnastics on a moving horse. A horse is lunged on a 38.5 ft to 46 ft (12 m to 14 m) circle by a team member while other members vault on and off the animal.

▶ *Team vaulting competitions involve riders carrying out six basic exercises. They are graded on how well and accurately these are performed.*

- **Most vaulting** exercises are performed at canter, although difficult maneuvers and some fun classes are performed at walk.

- **Horseball** is an increasingly popular game that involves leaning right out of the saddle toward the ground to pick up a small ball with a strapping harness.

- **Horseball** is a fast team game and points are scored by shooting the ball through a hoop.

- **Le Trec** is a fast-growing sport that involves three sections: orienteering, control (where the highest marks are awarded for the fastest walk and slowest canter), and an obstacle course.

- **In the obstacle section** of Le Trec, the rider faces hazards that might be met out hacking, for example, opening and closing a gate, jumping a log, or going down a steep slope.

- **Le Trec** stands for Technique de Randonnee Equestre de Competition and originated in France less than 30 years ago.

> ...FASCINATING FACT...
> Polocrosse is a cross between
> polo and lacrosse.

Preparing to compete

- **Whether the eventual goal** is to compete in a 50-mile ride or take part in a gymkhana game, the key to success is in preparation.

- **Before taking part** in any competitive activity, a horse should be fit, healthy, and up to the task.

- **It is up to the rider** to ensure that the horse is fully prepared for the job. This involves assessing its current state of fitness.

- **If a horse** has been turned away for several months, it needs to be brought back into work gradually. The tack needs to be checked for fit and the horse should be shod if necessary.

- **Light work** at walk should be slowly introduced. It is better to have four or five short sessions throughout a week than two longer workouts.

- **As the horse gains** condition, faster work such as trotting should be introduced and a variety of work should be undertaken, including hacking out and some school work.

- **When it is coping** well at canter and is responsive to the rider's aids, jumping can be reintroduced to the horse's routine.

- **If a gymkhana** is the goal, the pony should be introduced to some of the things it will experience at an event. For example, home-made flags can be used to accustom the pony to flags flapping. The pony and rider should also practice transitions in walk, trot, and canter.

- **If the goal** is to take part in dressage competitions the rider will need to learn the sequence of movements that make up the tests.

- **A good instructor** will help the horse and rider work toward their goal. Regular lessons and training will improve their skills and help them compete successfully.

▶ *Having access to a beach makes fitness training easier. The horse can be exercised on the sands and ridden through the water to cool off its legs.*

Dress codes

- **In showjumping competitions** the traditional attire is a hacking jacket or dark-colored riding jacket, white or cream jodhpurs, leather boots, a white shirt (worn with a tie) or a high-collared shirt for women, and a hat in black, brown, or navy.

- **Long hair** should be worn neatly in a hairnet. Gloves and body protectors are optional.

- **For dressage**, the rider should wear a hacking jacket or dark-colored riding jacket, depending on the level of competition. Black top hat and tails are only worn at advanced level.

- **Jodhpurs or breeches** are pale cream or white and while jodhpur boots can be worn at lower levels, long boots are expected at higher levels.

- **Depending on the type** of show class, the rider is expected to wear a hacking jacket, or black or navy riding jacket, white shirt, cream jodhpurs with brown or black boots and a black or navy hat.

- **Gloves** should be black, brown, or navy leather. The tie should not be too bright.

◀ *A hacking jacket is a tweedlike jacket that is cut to hang neatly while the rider is in the saddle.*

◀ *Long riding boots are traditionally made from leather but synthetic versions are available. Children and small adults can wear short ankle-length jodhpur boots.*

● **The cross-country stage** of eventing allows for greater individuality in what riders can wear. Riders wear a body protector and hard hat, carry a whip, and wear spurs. They usually wear brightly colored cross-country shirts that cover their arms.

● **In gymkhanas**, children generally wear cream jodhpurs, a riding hat, jodhpur boots, and possibly a body protector. They may wear a white shirt and pony club tie or a sweatshirt.

● **In western competitions**, riders usually wear a Stetson, a shirt, chaps, and leather boots.

● **Endurance riders** generally wear a cross-country or rugby shirt, jodhpurs or riding tights, jodhpur boots or riding trainers, half-chaps, gloves, safety hat. Body protectors are optional.

▶ *In the show ring, the top hat should be worn flat on the head, so that it sits just above the rider's eyebrows.*

165

Horses in history

- **The Greek general** Xenophon (427–354BC) wrote a book on horsemanship and riding which is credited with founding modern horsemanship. It was called *The Art of Horsemanship*.

- **Roman horsemen** were primarily used as messengers. Their job was to carry information from one area to another. The Romans protected their horses with body armor while fighting.

- **Chariot racing**, using between two and eight horses, was a popular entertainment in Roman times. The largest racetrack, Circus Maximus, held 250,000 people. Charioteers had to be prepared to cut themselves free of the reins if a chariot overturned while racing.

- **The Bayeux Tapestry** tells the story of the the Battle of Hastings in 1066. It shows the victory of mounted knights and archers over King Harold's English foot soldiers.

- **Knights and horses** have come to symbolize the Middle Ages. Knights followed a code of chivalry, which meant they had to behave honorably. The word chivalry is derived from the French *cheval*, meaning horse.

- **In tournaments**, knights risked their honor by attempting to defeat an opponent at a variety of competitions.

◀ *Jousting was a fight between two knights on horseback. Each knight tried to knock his opponent off his horse using a long lance.*

- **Heavy horses** were used in the Middle Ages as they were able to support the weight of an armored knight as well as their own body armor. A medieval war horse might have to carry up to 400 lb (180 kg).

- **The reins** of war horses were protected by metal plates to prevent the enemy from slicing through them.

- **The heavy war horse** was called a destrier. It stood at about 17 hh. Out of battle the knight rode a smaller, lighter horse called a palfrey. These horses were noted for their comfortable gait. They may also have owned a courser, which was a faster riding horse.

- **Stag hunting** on horses became popular in medieval times and the Norman term for starting up a stag became corrupted to the English phrase "tally-ho."

▲ *The Bayeux Tapestry includes 190 horses.*

Horses in war

- **Horses were important** in war because of their speed and agility and their ability to outmaneuver foot soldiers. It also meant messages and goods could be transported more quickly over greater distances.

- **In 330BC**, the cavalry of Alexander the Great rode over 400 mi (250 km) in only 11 days in pursuit of an enemy king.

- **The Roman cavalry** was made up of foreign soldiers who fought for Rome in return for goods.

- **The stirrup** was an important breakthrough when it was introduced to western Europe in the 8th century. It meant the rider had greater stability and could therefore use weapons more effectively.

- **North American Plains** Indians regarded horses as units of currency, and tribes fought over them. When the Nez Perce Indians, famous for their selective breeding of Appaloosas, were defeated by the US cavalry in 1877, their horses were almost wiped out.

- **The Duke of Wellington** rode his favorite horse, Copenhagen, at the Battle of Waterloo in 1815, when the English defeated the French. Emperor Napoleon's horse Marengo was captured by the British.

- **Horses were requisitioned** in Britain to support the fighting in World War I. It is thought that half a million horses were being used by the British military in France by 1916.

- **The role of the cavalry** was brought to an end with World War I. On the western front, the cavalry could not cope with trench warfare, barbed wire, or modern artillery and suffered massive casualties. It is estimated that about six million horses were used (one million of these were sent from the U.S.A.). Only a tiny proportion returned home.

- **The Trakehner** horse from Prussia was decimated as a breed during World War II when the horses were moved from eastern to western Europe.

- **The numbers of ponies** on Dartmoor in England were much reduced when the army took over the area for training during World War II.

▼ *Armor was worn by horse and rider during battle. It was heavy and this slowed the horse down but it provided vital protection.*

Horses at work

- **Prior to the Middle Ages**, oxen were used in agriculture work rather than horses.

- **Horse-drawn mail coaches** began running when roads were improved during the late 18th and early 19th century. Britain introduced the first mail coaches in 1784.

- **During the Golden Age of Coaching** (1815–45) it is estimated that about 150,000 horses were in service in England, pulling mail and stage coaches to transport passengers.

- **After the Industrial Revolution**, horses were used to transport goods into towns. They were used for many tasks: from carrying coffins at funerals to pulling rubbish carts.

- **Richard Martin** campaigned in England in the early 1820s for the more humane treatment of horses. They were often overworked, beaten, and neglected. In 1822, an Act of Parliament was passed to prevent the ill-treatment of animals, particularly cattle and horses. In 1824, the Society for the Prevention of Cruelty to Animals was formed (later to become the Royal Society) and a committee began to inspect slaughter houses and the conduct of coachmen in London.

- **The first trams** introduced were horse-drawn and traveled at 6 to 7 mph (9 to 11 km/h). New York was the first city to introduce the horse-drawn tram in 1832.

- **Horses were also used** to pull narrow boats along the canal systems in Britain. These horses were known as barge horses or boaters. They walked along the tow paths beside the canals.

- **Pit ponies** were widely used in the mining industry in Britain. In 1913, there were 70,000 pit ponies. Although numbers were very much reduced, ponies were still being used in some mines as late as the 1990s.

- **When formal grass lawns** were first introduced into England in the 1700s, they were kept short by grazing animals and workers with hand tools. The first cylinder mowers were invented in the 1800s. They were pulled by horses wearing leather boots to avoid damaging the grass.

- **The need for the horse** in all areas of transportation, agriculture, and communication existed until man invented alternative mechanized means of achieving the same ends. Horses were replaced with trains, tractors, cars, buses, lorries, and trams. The pulling power of an engine is still described in terms of horsepower. One horsepower is equivalent to 745 watts.

▼ *Machinery, such as this seed drill, designed to be used by horses improved the speed and efficiency of farming.*

171

Horses in public service

- **Mounted police** are used worldwide, the most famous being the Royal Canadian Mounted Police (RCMP) who formed in 1873. The North-West Mounted Police Force were established to stop the trade in alcohol amongst Native American Indians and collect customs, as well as carrying out normal police duties.

- **Today**, the RCMP's role is largely ceremonial. Their horses are black, heavy Thoroughbred types and stand about 16 hh to 17 hh.

- **The Mounties** created a musical ride to show off their considerable riding ability and to entertain the public.

- **One of their formations** called the "dome" was featured on a 50 dollar Canadian bill.

- **Each year**, foals born in the Mounties' stables have names beginning with the same letter.

- **The first mounted police** force in Britain was the London Bow Street Horse Patrol in 1760.

◀ *This horse is wearing a ceremonial bridle based on a traditional military design decorated with ornate brass fixings.*

▲ *The Mounties' musical ride consists of a series of movements ridden at speed.*

- **Police horses** are trained to ignore missiles, crowds, and sudden noise and learn how to step over obstacles thrown in their path.

- **Police horses** provide support to the rest of the police force, particularly when there is a danger to public safety at demonstrations, or events where there are a large number of people.

- **In England**, the Thames Valley Police Mounted Section patrol royal and parliamentary occasions. Each horse has two names. One is an official name, such as a town or city of the region; the other is its stable name. For example, Chequers is also known as Corky.

...FASCINATING FACT...
The last US army horse died in 1976
aged 29. He was called Black Jack.

173

Horses in literature

- *Black Beauty*, written in 1877 by Anna Sewell, tells the story of a horse and his companions.

- *My Friend Flicka*, *Thunderhead* and *The Green, Green Grass of Wyoming* were three classic novels written by Mary O' Hara in the 1940s, featuring life on an American ranch.

- **The highwayman** Dick Turpin, who was hanged in 1739 for robbery and horse theft, rode a mare called Black Bess. In a book called *Rookwood* written by Harrison Ainsworth in 1834, Dick Turpin rides his horse from London to York.

- **In Robert Burns' poem** *Tam o' Shanter*, the drunk has to place his faith in his horse Meg to help him flee from angry witches. As they reach safety by crossing a stream, the witches catch hold of the mare's tail.

- **Shakespeare's** *Richard III* has the well-known line "A horse, a horse, my kingdom for a horse."

◀ *Several film adaptations of Anna Sewell's novel* Black Beauty *have been produced. This scene is from the 1994 version.*

- **The poem** *The Charge of the Light Brigade* by Alfred, Lord Tennyson commemorates the Battle of Balaclava during the Crimean War in 1854.

- **The Trojan Horse** was built by the ancient Greeks and left outside the besieged city of Troy during the Trojan Wars around 1185BC. Believing the giant wooden horse was a gift, the Trojans brought it into the city. However, the Greeks had cleverly tricked the Trojans. After nightfall, they left their hiding place inside the horse and opened the city gates to allow their army access. The Trojans were then defeated.

- ***Don Quixote de la Mancha*** was the creation of the Spanish poet Miguel de Cervantes in the 17th century. Don Quixote rode a horse called Rosinante and was accompanied on his travels by his friend Sancho Panza.

- **In Jonathan Swift's** *Gulliver's Travels,* written in 1726, creatures called houyhnhnms appear. They were civilized talking horses.

- **The Pullein-Thompson sisters**, Christine, Diana and Josephine, were prolific writers of horse and pony books for children. They began writing in the 1940s while still in their teens. With their brother they ran a family riding school at the same time.

▶ *The Trojan horse was an enormous wooden horse built by the ancient Greeks during the Trojan Wars.*

175

Women and horses

- **Lady Isobel Blunt** (1837–1917) was the first English woman to visit the Arabian peninsula. She loved Arab horses and together with her husband set up a stud in Egypt.

- **Calamity Jane** (1852–1903) was born in Missouri. Her real name was Martha Jane Canary. She toured the country in Wild West shows and was skilled at riding and shooting.

- **Mrs Christian Davies** (1667–1739), was from Dublin, Ireland. Also known as Mother Ross, she rode through Flanders disguised as a man in search of her husband who was fighting in battle. After taking part in the fighting, she managed to find him, but he later died in battle.

- **Emily Davison** (1872–1913) was a suffragette who was killed when she tried to catch hold of the king's horse during the Derby races. Wearing a "Women's Social and Political Union" banner, she was trampled beneath the horse's legs and died a few days later.

- **Alicia Meynell** was the first female jockey to ride in an official horse race. In 1804, she competed in a four-mile race in York, England.

- **Celia Fiennes** (1662–1741) was an English travel writer who recorded her diaries in the late 17th and early 18th centuries. Her diaries *Through England On a Side Saddle in the Time of William and Mary* were first published in 1888.

- **Annie Oakley** (1860–1926) was an American rodeo star and sharp shooter who appeared in Buffalo Bill's Wild West Touring Show.

- **Born in 1953**, Lucinda Prior-Palmer from England was an outstanding event rider. She won the prestigious Badminton Horse Trials six times between 1973 and 1984.

- **Pat Smythe** (1928–96) was Britain's first Olympic woman rider and the most successful female showjumper of her time. She won a bronze medal in the 1956 Olympics.

- **Adele Theodore** (1835–68), an American actress, is remembered for appearing near naked on horseback in shows around the U.S.A. in the 1860s.

▼ *Annie Oakley was famed for her accurate shooting—even when moving at speed on horseback.*

Horses in the spotlight

- *National Velvet* was a 1944 film starring Elizabeth Taylor. Adapted from the novel by Enid Bagnold, Velvet Brown rides her horse to victory in the Grand National, but is later disqualified when officials discover she is a girl and therefore not allowed to enter the race.

- **The 2003 film** *Seabiscuit* tells the story of an American racehorse who became a champion and national hero.

- **Mr Ed** the "Talking Horse," was a much loved palomino who appeared in a 1960s television series. In the programme he could talk, but only to his carer, and this resulted in many difficult and funny predicaments.

- **Gene Autrey** was a famous singing cowboy during the 1930s, 40s and 50s. He featured in many film stunts with his horse Champion.

- **Norman Thelwell** (1923–2004) created cartoons of round, fat ponies and child riders in amusing situations. The cartoons have been popular since the 1950s.

▲ *Champion the Wonder Horse was played on screen by a number of different horses. The first "Champion" died in 1943.*

◀ *Seabiscuit (1933–47) was an unlikely racing prospect. A long shot that became a legend, his story was told in a 2003 film.*

● **Roy Rogers** and his horse Trigger were media stars. Trigger performed many publicity stunts such as signing into hotels using a pencil held between his teeth. He appeared in 90 films and over 100 television shows.

● **Robert Redford** starred in and directed the 1998 film *The Horse Whisperer*. In it he treats a horse that has been badly traumatized in an accident.

● **Buffalo Bill Cody** featured a horse called Sultan in his Wild West shows in the 1880s.

● *On White Horses* was the theme tune to a popular children's television program in the 1960s. The show featured Lipizzaner horses that were trained at a stud farm.

```
....FASCINATING FACT....
Shadowfax, the greatest of the horses of Rohan,
was Gandalf's horse in Tolkien's Lord of the Rings.
```

The Wild West

- **The Plains Indians** branded their horses with identifying marks to signify which horses belonged to which tribe. Their horses were bred from Spanish horses.

- **Horses were important** to North American Indians as they offered greater mobility and a way of transporting goods more easily. They were also used in war and for hunting.

- **The North American Indians** believed that particular patterns on their colored horses represented magical properties that would protect them in battle. The Shishoni Indians hung precious objects around their horses' necks.

▲ *Although they have been romanticized in movies and television, a cowboy's work was essentially to move large herds of cattle through the prairies.*

◀ *Cowboys wore chaps over their pants to protect their legs while riding. These could be made from goat, bear, or sheep skin.*

● **A cowboy's most prized** possession was his saddle. Even if he gambled away everything else including his horse, he would retain the saddle and carry it on his back.

● **The Sioux Indians** painted horses on their tepees and made halters and ropes out of horsehair and buffalo hide.

● **The Crow Indians** were famed for their horse skills, both as horse whisperers and as exceptional riders.

● **Wild Bill Hickok**, was born in 1812 in Illinois. A gunman and a sheriff, he also acted as a scout for the US cavalry. He was killed by a bullet in the back during a card game in 1876.

● **The Pony Express** mail service began in 1860, traveling between St Joseph, Missouri and San Francisco. Within two years the service was replaced by stage coaches.

● **Gauchos of Argentina** are the South American equivalent of the North American cowboy. Skilled horsemen, it is said that if a gaucho is without a horse he is without legs.

> ...FASCINATING FACT...
> Indian warriors painted their horses for protection and courage.
> The symbols could be hand prints, stripes, or animal designs.

Myths and legends

- **The four horsemen** of the Apocalypse are said to signify the end of the world. Conquest rides a white horse, Famine a black one, War a red one, and Plague a pale-colored horse. They are seen as the four evils of the world.

- **Pegasus**, the winged horse in Greek mythology, carried Zeus' thunderbolt. He was born from the blood of Medusa the Gorgon.

- **In Norse mythology**, Odin the god of war had an eight-legged horse called Sleipnir who could gallop faster than any other horse, and travel across the sky and the sea.

- **The unicorn** is a mythical beast that has the body of a pure white horse with a twisted horn on its head. It symbolizes goodness and purity.

▲ *The horn of the unicorn was believed to be able to neutralize poison.*

> ...FASCINATING FACT...
> In Roman times, white horses were a
> symbol of the gods and power.

- **According to Arabian legend**, the god Allah created the Arab horse "out of a handful of the southern wind."

- **In Irish mythology**, the horse was believed to carry souls of the dead from this world to the next.

- **Poseidon**, the Greek god of the sea, rode a chariot drawn by fabulous half-horse half-fish creatures.

- **Kelpies** feature in Scottish mythology. These creatures are associated with running water. They attract unwary people towards deep water by appearing as a beautiful human then drag their victim underwater while taking on the form of a water horse.

- **In Greek mythology**, the gods of the sun and moon rode chariots across the sky each dawn and dusk.

▶ *Centaurs were half-man half-horse. They had the head and torso of a man, attached to the back and legs of a horse.*

Horses in art

- **Cave paintings** depicting horses involved in hunting have been found in Europe. They are thought to date back to around 15000BC.

- **Pictish stone** carvings of sea horses still stand in Scotland. These stones are believed to date back to AD400–700.

▲ *Early cave paintings were drawn using earth or carbon mixed with water or animal fat.*

- **A terracotta army** of life-size figures was discovered in Xi'an in China in the early 20th century. Sculptures of horses and bronze chariots were also buried in the tomb of the first Chinese emperor more than 2,000 years ago.

- **Rosa Bonheur** (1832–99) was a French painter who specialized in horses and is noted for the detail in her work. She painted the famous *Horse Fair* in 1853.

- **Theodore Gericault** (1791–1824) was a keen horseman and painter. Tragically the French artist died as a result of a horse riding accident.

- **George Stubbs** (1724–1806) was a popular English painter closely associated with horses in art. He made a painstaking study of the anatomy of horses and published a book called *The Anatomy of the Horse* in 1766. *Whistlejacket*, painted in 1762, is a famous example of his work.

- **Leonardo da Vinci** (1452–1519), famous for painting the *Mona Lisa*, also made detailed anatomical drawings of horses.

- **The Flemish painter** Anthony Van Dyck (1599–1641) depicted Charles I on horseback in 1637–38. The lifesize work shows Charles, a small man, as powerful and impressive.

- **Russian-born** Vassily Kandinsky (1866–1944) and the German Franz Marc (1880–1916) founded a group of artists in 1911 called Der Blaue Reiter (The Blue Rider). Franz Marc painted *The Large Blue Horses* in the same year.

- **Elizabeth Frink** (1930–93) was an English sculptor whose early work included a series of horse and rider sculptures.

▲ Man on Horseback
by Sir Anthony Van Dyck.

Horse folklore

- **Horseshoes** are often fixed onto buildings and stable doors as they are thought to bring good luck.

- **A myth exists** that Lady Godiva rode naked through the town of Coventry, England in the 11th century, on a gray horse to protest at taxes.

- *Ride a Cock-horse* is a traditional English folk rhyme. It is believed to relate to Queen Elizabeth I of England and tells the story of how she traveled to the town of Banbury.

- **Rutland Castle** in England has a tradition where visiting lords have to present a horseshoe to the castle.

▲ *Horseshoes have traditionally been the symbol of good luck.*

◄ *Horse brasses have intricate patterns often showing different symbols of luck.*

- **Horses brasses**, metal ornaments that are attached to heavy agricultural horses' harnesses, are often considered to be lucky.

- **Giant white horses** are carved in chalk on some hillsides in England. The county of Wiltshire is home to more than ten of these carvings, some dating back hundreds of years.

- **Folklore stories** say that when King Arthur of the Round Table returns to the throne one of the chalk horses will get up and dance.

- **An Irish folk cure** for toothache suggests rubbing the affected area of the jaw with a dead horse's tooth to relieve the pain.

- **According to Arabian folklore**, the chestnut horse is the fastest and bravest of all horses.

- **In Celtic folklore** it is said to be bad luck to cross the path of plowing horses.

▼ *Some people believe that the chalk carvings originally commemorated King Alfred's victory over the Danes in the 9th century.*

Famous horses

- **Man o' War** was a famous American racehorse who began racing in 1919. He won 20 out of 21 races.

- **According to the historian** Plutarch, Alexander the Great tamed his horse Bucephalus. The animal then carried Alexander into many battles.

▶ *John Whitaker riding Milton. The horse was the first showjumper to win £1 million in prize money.*

- **Foxhunter** was a 16.3 hh showjumper ridden by Sir Harry Llewellyn, and they won an Olympic medal for Great Britain. Foxhunter died aged 19 in 1959.

- **Red Rum** won the Grand National three times in the 1970s. He died in 1995 at the age of 30 and is buried at Aintree race course in England.

- **The Spanish soldier** Rodrigo Diaz de Vivar (1040–99), better known as El Cid, rode a white horse called Babieca.

- **Arkle** has been described as the greatest steeplechaser ever. Born in 1957, he raced during the 1960s and died in 1970.

- **Shergar**, a famous racehorse in the 1980s was kidnapped from a stud in Ireland in 1983. Never recovered, his disappearance remains a mystery.

- **Stroller** was a 14.2-hh pony ridden by British rider Marion Coakes in the 1968 Olympic Games. He was the only pony to have competed at this level and they won the silver medal.

- **Comanche** was the only U.S. cavalry horse to survive the Battle of Little Bighorn or Custer's Last Stand in 1876. Comanche was injured but recovered from his wounds and became a national hero. He lived until he was 29, dying in 1891.

> ...FASCINATING FACT...
> In 1947, the funeral of the racehorse
> Man o' War was attended by 2,000 people.

Royal riders

- **Queen Boudicca of the Iceni**, famous for leading an uprising against the Romans in England around AD60, was a keen horse breeder. It is believed that she exported some horses to Rome.

- **King Alexander III of Scotland** died in 1286 when he rode his horse over a cliff in Fife during the night.

- **Princess Anne of Bohemia** is credited with making the side saddle popular in England after she married Richard II in 1381.

- **Henry VIII** (1497–1543) was presented with a highly ornate set of Burgundian horse armor that covered the horse's neck, face, and body by the Holy Roman Emperor Maximilian I around 1510.

- **A keen horseman** in his youth, Henry VIII is said to have tired out up to ten horses while out hunting for the day. He suffered a permanently damaged leg at the age of 44 when a horse rolled over on him at a tournament.

- **His daughter** Elizabeth I was said to have been a very able horsewoman who rode faster than her male contemporaries.

▶ *Boudicca was a keen horsewoman. This shows her standing aboard a horse-drawn chariot.*

···FASCINATING FACT···
The Ascot racecourse in England was built
in 1711 on the orders of Queen Anne.

- **After the death** of Oliver Cromwell, Charles II returned to England in 1660 and reinstated horse racing, which had been banned. He expanded the center at Newmarket and even took part in races himself, under the alias "Old Rowley."

- **Queen Elizabeth II** has been an able horsewoman since a child and has an active interest in horse racing. Her husband, HRH The Duke of Edinburgh, has also been a keen polo player and competed in driving competitions.

- **Princess Anne**, the Princess Royal, took part in the three-day team event for Britain in the Olympics of 1976.

▶ *Queen Elizabeth II has attended the Trooping the Colour ceremony every year since the start of her reign in 1952, except in 1955 when the parade was cancelled due to a national rail strike.*

191

Horse trivia

▲ *Competition horses can be taught to tackle obstacles they would naturally avoid. This horse and rider are confidently negiotiating the steep Derby Bank at Hickstead.*

- **A horse's knee joint** is equivalent to a human wrist and its hock joint, the ankle.

- **A horse wearing** a green ribbon on its tail is young and inexperienced. A red ribbon is a warning to other riders that the horse might kick out.

- **The largest horse museum** in the world is the International Museum of the Horse in Lexington, Kentucky.

- **As a horse ages**, its joints stiffen and the hollows above its eyes become more prominent. The backbone also becomes more pronounced.

- **Horses start to age** from their mid-teens and usually live until they are between 25 and 35 years old. A 16-year-old horse is about 50 years old in human terms. Ponies generally live longer; there are records of them living well into their 50s.

- **The average length** of a horses stride at walk is 5 ft 6 in to 6 ft (1.67 m to 1.83 m).

- **A horse has** approximately 60 ft (18 m) of small intestine and 20 ft (6 m) of large intestine.

- **Normal horse droppings** are at least 15 percent water.

- **Horses can detect** both higher and lower sound ranges than humans.

> ...FASCINATING FACT...
> A horse's heart weighs about 8.8 lb (4 kg).

Body talk

- **The normal temperature** for a horse at rest is 101°F to 101.5°F (38.3°C to 38.6°C).

- **A horse can see** a moving object clearly, but has difficulty determining the distance between objects.

- **It is not clear** from research which colors a horse can see.

- **A horse can sleep** standing up because of a locking mechanism in its leg.

- **There are about** one million horses in the UK today.

- **Horse blankets** usually increase in size in 3 in (8 cm) increments. To find a horse's blanket size, a measurement is taken from the mid point of its chest to the edge of its flanks.

- **On average**, a horse has drowsy periods that total between two and four hours a day.

- **An ergot** is a small horny growth found at the back of a horse's fetlock join.

- **Grass sickness** is a disease affecting the nerves controlling a horse's gut. It can be fatal.

▶ *A well-fitted blanket should fit snugly around the neck, while allowing for plenty of shoulder movement.*

> **...FASCINATING FACT...**
> In warm countries, horses are said to enjoy
> oranges, grapefruit, and dates.

▼ *Horses not only groom a bonded partner, but will often try to groom their carer while being brushed.*

Facts and figures

- **At the peak period** of feeding, a nursing mare can produce up to 32 pt (18 lt) of milk per day.

- **A horse uses** about 80 percent of the energy gained from food in keeping warm.

- **Horses generally find** it soothing to have their ears gently rubbed.

- **Horses have seven** common blood types and can be used as blood donors for other horses.

- **Horses' bodies** consist of 65 percent water. This equates to 9 gal per 100 lb (40 lt per 100 kg).

▶ *A nursing mare will need to drink extra water to replace the fluid used to feed her foal.*

▶ *These mares and foals are enjoying cantering around in their paddock. Each canter stride includes a moment of suspension.*

- **Horses produce** up to 2.5 gal (10 lt) of urine daily.

- **To check** if a horse is hydrated, press the gum above an incisor until it becomes pale. The area should should turn pink again after one to two seconds if the animal is healthy and hydrated.

- **The length** of a horse's stride is measured between two successive imprints of the same foot.

- **Cantering** is a three-speed gait: 1–2–3, 1–2–3.

. . . FASCINATING FACT . . .
When cantering, a horse takes a
breath every stride.

197

Terminology

- **Napping** is the refusal by the horse or pony to do what its rider asks. Symptoms may include refusal to leave other horses or to move forward, bucking, and rearing.

- **The bit** is the mouthpiece, usually made of metal, which is placed in a horse's mouth.

- **A martingale** is an item of tack that is designed to prevent the horse raising its head too high. It is attached to the reins, has a neckstrap, and a central piece running under the horse's chest and between its legs to fix onto the girth.

▲ *A numnah or saddle cloth is usually placed underneath an English-style saddle to provide extra comfort for the horse's back. Regular washing is needed to maintain hygiene.*

- **A breastplate** stops a saddle slipping backwards. It has a loop that fits over the horse's neck and side straps fixed to the saddle. A central strap attaches to the girth.

...·FASCINATING FACT·...
Metal bits were first used for horses
between 1300 and 1200BC

Jointed Pelham

Eggbutt snaffle

Loose-ring snaffle

● **The horn** and cantle are the highest points at the front and back of a western saddle.

● **A livery or a boarding stable** is a stable yard where horseowners pay a professional to look after their horses, on a full-time or part-time basis.

● **A hack** is a ride out that should be enjoyable for both horse and rider.

● **A menage** is an arena that is used for riding and schooling horses.

● **Bots** are flies that lay eggs on a horse's skin. If swallowed, the larvae develop in the stomach and are passed as droppings from which further flies emerge.

Liverpool driving bit

Four-ring gag

◀ *Bits are available in many different styles but all have rings or cheek pieces on each side to stop them sliding through the horse's mouth.*

199

Horse talk

- **Cast** describes a horseshoe that is lost or comes off accidentally. It can also refer to a horse that gets stuck while lying down.

- **To change the rein** means to change direction. A riding instructor will often request that the rein is changed at a certain point in the school, which is identified by letter markers.

- **A lasso** is a long rope with a loop at the end used to catch cattle and other animals.

- **A saddle-rack** is a wooden or metal support on which a saddle is stored when not being used.

- **A pressure halter** teaches a horse not to pull away from its handler, by applying pressure to the nose and poll area.

- **Poles**, both colored and plain, are used in a variety of ways to train horses to be aware of their bodies and feet. They can be placed in patterns and the horse asked to walk through them, used as trotting poles, or as take off points while jumping.

- **Quarter marks** are used to show off the good condition of a show horse's coat. They can be applied by using special plastic stencil sheets or by using a fine comb.

▲ *The lasso is secured around the western saddle horn when the rider dismounts to deal with a roped animal. A lariat is a type of lasso.*

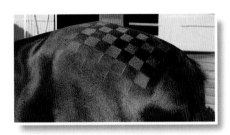

◀ *Quarter marks are popular for some types of show horse. They are achieved by brushing the hair in different ways to make a pattern.*

- **Spooky** is used to describe a horse who is liable to shy or start away from an object that is unfamiliar or frightening.

- **Turn out** describes the area where a horse is grazed and allowed to move about freely.

- **Warbles** are caused by warble flies that lay eggs on a horse's coat. The larvae penetrate the skin to make obvious and painful lumps.

▼ *Horses enjoy the freedom of being turned out in a field.*

Equine terms

- **Irons** are another name for stirrups.

- **Electrolytes** are minerals and salts found in the horse's body. Supplements can be given to a horse to help replace those lost from excess sweating.

- **Forage** is the term for bulk food, such as hay, haylage, or grass, and should form the basis for all equine feeding programs.

- **Ad lib** is a term often used in relation to forage. It means that forage is always available to the horse and it is not rationed.

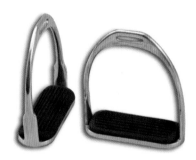

▲ *These stirrups have safety treads that offer the rider better grip.*

- **Schooling** is the term used when a horse is being trained to learn and obey specific commands called aids.

- **A schoolmaster** is a horse that is calm and obedient and will obey commands correctly.

◄ *When hay is fed from a hay net, care must be taken to ensure that it is tied tightly at a suitable height so that the horse does not pull it from the wall or get its legs entangled in the net.*

- **Gait** is another word for pace. A horse usually has four basic gaits: walk, trot, canter, and gallop. Some breeds have other gaits, such as the Icelandic Horse's *tölt*— a four-beat running walk.

- **The "inside leg"** refers to whichever leg is nearest the center of a circle when a horse is being schooled in a ring.

- **Branding** is a method of permanently marking a horse, so that it can be identified.

- **Haw** is the word for a horse's third eyelid. It is a thin membrane of skin that can be drawn over the eye.

▶ *Headcollars are available in leather or webbing.*

Horse loves

- **Horses enjoy** being able to pick at food over a long period of time.

- **Horses who get along** will stand grooming each other, nibbling the skin at the base of each other's withers.

- **Rolling** on the ground after exercise is pleasurable to a horse.

- **Horses enjoy routine.** They like to be fed at regular times and to be kept near familiar companions.

- **The freedom to graze** and roam around at will is enjoyed by horses.

- **Horses love company**—preferably that of other horses.

▲ *Horses enjoy rolling and it helps circulation and skin condition.*

▶ *Good grazing offers horses a choice of grasses and herbs. Horses are fussy eaters and will disregard weeds, such as docks and thistles.*

- **Horses often like a bath** if the weather is really hot. They can be sponged and hosed down to cool them off.

- **Horses prefer the familiar** and may be reluctant to try a new route or ride out on their own if they are used to being ridden in company.

- **Scratching up against trees** or stable walls is enjoyed by most horses. They sometimes even try to use humans as rubbing posts.

- **Horses usually prefer** to be stroked rather than patted.

Horse hates

- **Horses hate** to be tied up too tightly, so they cannot move their heads or look around.

- **Stones in horses' feet** cause discomfort. Small stones and sharp twigs can puncture the hoof sole and create abscesses and lameness.

- **Being startled** or approached quickly from behind may cause a horse to kick out. Any unexpected incident or occurence may cause a horse to spook or react in an unpredictable way.

- **Horses will become bored** if left for lengthy periods of time in a stable. This may cause behavioral problems.

- **Horses hate** to be chased.

- **Horses do not enjoy continuous rain.** If their coat becomes soaked through, they may develop sores on their skin. This is called rain scald and is similar to mud fever that affects the heels and legs.

- **Ill-fitting tack** will cause a horse distress. Regular checks should be made to ensure it is not causing any discomfort to the horse.

- **Horses dislike riders** who pull on their mouths and are unbalanced in the saddle.

```
...FASCINATING FACT...
Many horses are said to be
frightened of pigs.
```

- **Mares will become distressed** if separated from their foals. They will repeatedly call for them if weaning is carried out unsympathetically.

▲ *A horse's first reaction to danger is to flee. With its ears laid back, this horse is exhibiting signs of anxiety .*

Index

Index

Index

Index

Index

Index

Index

Index

Acknowledgments

The publishers would like to thank the following artists
who have contributed to this book:
Steve Caldwell (Allied Artists), Jim Channel, Terry Gabbey, Sally Holmes,
Richard Hook (Linden Artists), Janos Marffy, Angus McBride, Andrea Morandi,
Terry Riley, Peter Sarson, Rudi Vizi, Mike White (Temple Rogers)

The publishers would like to thank the following sources
for the use of their photographs:
Page 14 (Centaur Summer Storm) Jenny Deakin; 25 Melissa Brotherwood;
30 Jenny Deakin; 34 Shires Equestrian Products; 36 Janice Boyd; 37 Karl Norman;
42/43 E Jeffries and Sons Ltd; 44 Karl Norman; 45 E Jeffries and Sons Ltd;
46 Shires Equestrian Products; 49 Shires Equestrian Products; 50 Lisa Clayden;
52/53/54 Horseware Ireland; 55 Ifor Williams Trailers Ltd; 56 Horseware Ireland;
57 Shires Equestrian Products; 58/59/61 Karl Norman; 63/65 Lisa Clayden;
67 Bob Langrish; 68(t) Shires Equestrian products; 71 Horseware Ireland;
73 Chart Stables Ltd; 74 Bob Langrish; 78 Lisa Clayden; 79 Nokia; 82 Lisa Clayden;
83 Shires Equestrian Products; 85 Bob Langrish; 87/88 Shires Equestrian Products;
89/90/92/97 Bob Langrish; 98 Acquire Image Media; 100 Bob Langrish;
104/108/110 Acquire Image Media; 111 Lisa Clayden; 112 (Evergreen Hamlet) Nicholas
Pound; 113 (Moorcorner Minstrel II) Nicholas Pound; 114 (Lowhouses Black Magic)
Nipna Stud; 115 (Inglegarth Illustrious/Townend Aaron) Janice Boyd; 116/126
Bob Langrish; 131 (Kvaals Aida) Dawn Thorpe; 139 Ifor Williams Trailers Ltd; 143(t)
(Lingjohn Juniper) Nipna Stud; 143(b) Shires Equestrian Products; 150 Bob Langrish;
159 AFP/EPA/DPA/Carsten Rehder/Getty Images; 160 Bob Langrish; 162/165 Shires
Equestrian Products; 174 Warner/pictorialpress.com; 178 Flying A/pictorialpress.com;
179 Universal/Dreamworks/pictorialpress.com; 188 Bob Langrish; 194 Shires
Equestrian Products; 198 Horseware Ireland; 199 E J Jeffries and Sons Ltd;
200/201 Shires Equestrian Products; 202(t) E J Jeffries and Sons Ltd; 202(b)
Shires Equestrian Products; 203 Horseware Ireland; 204 Lisa Clayden

All other images from Miles Kelly Archives,
Corel, digitalvision, DigitalSTOCK, PhotoDisc